D0597909

TAKE
BACK
YOUR
LIFE!

H. Dale Burke

HARVEST HOUSE PUBLISHERS

EUGENE, OREGON

Unless otherwise indicated all Scripture quotations are taken from the New American Standard Bible ®, © 1960, 1962, 1963, 1968, 1971, 1972, 1973, 1975, 1977, 1995 by The Lockman Foundation. Used by permission. (www.Lockman.org)

Verses marked NIV are taken from the HOLY BIBLE, NEW INTERNATIONAL VERSION®. NIV®. Copyright © 1973, 1978, 1984 by the International Bible Society. Used by permission of Zondervan. All rights reserved.

Cover by Koechel Peterson & Associates, Inc., Minneapolis, Minnesota

H. Dale Burke: Published in association with Eames Literary Services, Nashville, Tennessee.

Italicized text in Scripture quotations indicates author's emphasis.

TAKE BACK YOUR LIFE!

Copyright © 2007 by H. Dale Burke
Published by Harvest House Publishers
Eugene, Oregon 97402
www.harvesthousepublishers.com

Library of Congress Cataloging-in-Publication Data
Burke, H. Dale, 1953-
Take back your life! / H. Dale Burke.
    p. cm.
ISBN-13: 978-0-7369-1400-0 (ppk.)
ISBN-10: 0-7369-1400-5
1. Simplicity—Religious aspects—Christianity. 2. Time management—Religious aspects—Christianity. 3. Control (Psychology)—Religious aspects—Christianity. I. Title.
BV4647.S48B87 2007
248.4—dc22

                                                                                    2006026958

All rights reserved. No part of this publication may be reproduced, stored in a retrieval system, or transmitted in any form or by any means—electronic, mechanical, digital, photocopy, recording, or any other—except for brief quotations in printed reviews, without the prior permission of the publisher.

Printed in the United States of America

07 08 09 10 11 12 13 14 15 / LB-SK / 10 9 8 7 6 5 4 3 2 1

CONTENTS

To my three children—Beth, Paul, and Jaime

As I finish this book, for the first time in my life, I write from the proverbial "empty nest." You are all now out of college, out of the house, married to great and godly spouses, walking with God, and pursuing your own God-given dreams. Your mother and I could not be more proud of the three, indeed now the *six,* of you!

For 26 years, exactly half of my life, you gave me three great reasons to never give up the struggle to "take back *my* life." You made me a better man as I sought to be a better dad.

To my wife, Becky

Thank you for always being the number one reason I have to come home at the end of the day. You not only motivate me to "take back *my* life," you help make it happen. Thanks for all the love and respect, encouragement and support, and forgiveness and grace you've given me for 32 wonderful years. May our now-empty nest be filled with even more love, big dreams, and the joy of our grandchildren!

Take Back Your Life!

My life feels out of control. Yes, I can tell I'm alive, breathing, walking, and talking my way through each day. But I keep feeling like I'm not the one calling the shots! I'm at the mercy of my own life, the life I created. It may be *my* creation, but now this creature, My Life (like the monster in Frankenstein) has come to life and taken over (you guessed it) my life! Do you ever feel like Your Life has taken over your life? Let me explain before you think I've lost my mind like some mad scientist.

It didn't start that way. Years ago I remember having a life and living it just as I chose to live it. Of course that was when I was about four years of age. Those glorious preschool years were spent just the way I planned them! But from then on, my life began to build the monster—slowly but surely, My Life began to come together. Now don't get me wrong; it came together pretty much according to my design, my blueprint. I went to school, made the grades, played sports, met the girl of my dreams, got my education (even with honors), married the girl, got my masters (again with honors), and got my first real job. No more school, a wonderful wife, and a job I loved. My Life was taking shape, and I liked what was on the table!

But then something happened. I succeeded. Or, as a Christian, I should say more accurately, I was blessed. Every part of my life began to expand exponentially. I prayed for a family, and suddenly it happened. My wife, Becky, announced, "I'm pregnant!" I now had a new label—*dad*. Not only was my family expanding, my career began to take off. My church (I forgot to say my first job was as a pastor of a new university church) began to attract more and more new families who needed a spiritual home. Don't get me wrong—I prayed for the church to grow, and God answered my prayer. At work and at home everything was multiplying and expanding. Even my waistline began to...well, let's not go there! You get the picture. God blessed, and I got busy. And busier. And busier.

That's when I began to first notice that My Life was coming to life and taking control. As I got busier, God continued to bless and my responsibilities became greater. Before long I began to travel more, speak more, and pick up the pace as I tried to care for a growing church and family (three kids now). And don't forget the wonderful wife God gave to me. She needed more help because the kids now outnumbered mom and dad. My Life was growing bigger and stronger as the weeks flew by. It (this monster is gender neutral affecting men and women alike) began to tell me what to do, when to do it, and to scold me if I didn't get it all done to Its satisfaction. My Life was setting the agenda and calling the shots, and I began to feel less and less in control. Something had to change or this monster of my own creation would rule and then ruin everything.

At times I was tempted to "just say no" to the demands It was placing on me. But most of Its demands were good, not evil. It was telling me to serve my wife, my kids, my friends, and especially the members of my church. After all, I was their pastor. I was the shepherd, and they were the sheep. Wasn't it my job to care for their needs? Wasn't this actually God's will for my life? If I were in business, they would have been my customers. If I were in management, they would have been my employees. This was, after all, My Life, and I was glad It was growing. But I was losing my joy.

The questions I was facing—the challenges we all face in today's high-demand world—were, How can we succeed without becoming failures? Is it possible to chase our dreams and still sleep well at night? How can we keep the blessings from becoming burdens? And if It, Your Life, has already grown up and taken over, how can you "take It back" and then keep It serving you instead of you serving It?

> **LIFE BEHAVES BEST WHEN IT IS UNDER GOD'S CONTROL.**

This book is about taming the monster called Life. If you feel the Life you've created has taken over and started calling the shots and forcing your choices, then this book is for you. If you are tired of always running and never catching up, then this book is for you. It is time to take back your life.

Here's the good news: It *is* possible to harness the creature and return it to its rightful place. But it won't be easy. You'll have to learn a new way of thinking, a new way of living, and it doesn't just come naturally. It will take the help of others, a team effort, and most of all, God. He loves you and wants your Life under control—your control, and then His control. Yes, life behaves best when it is under God's control. But here's the dilemma: How can I give to God what I don't even possess? If my day from dawn to dusk is being driven by My Life rather than myself, then I can't even give it to God. After all, it is out of my control. So what can I do?

Let's start by taking a closer look at why this Monster, My Life, is so hard to capture and control.

Life is too fast...so let's *slow it down.*

It's time we put some serious effort into slowing down our lives—not so much that we drop out of the race and abandon our dreams, but enough to reduce the sense of hurriedness we always feel. The Monster thrives when life is being lived in "hurry mode." Our society lives on the brink of burnout.

Even today's soccer moms feel it. They rush from school dance lessons to the practice field and then to church by way of the kid's favorite drive-thru for dinner! How can we restore the discipline of rest in our lives so that we're not always feeling frazzled? How can we feel refreshed as we go into a new day or new week? We're going to find out in the pages ahead. To take back your life, slow It down!

Life is too complex...so let's *simplify it.*

The creature grows bigger and stronger as life gets more and more complex. One lesson we'll learn in this book is how to simplify life. We must face the fact that one of our key problems is that we are trying to do too much. My Life says, "You *must* do it all and please *everyone*." Whether you are working or retired, single or married, building a family or a business, life is too complex. You can't do it all, and you will *never* please *everyone*.

One of the principles I teach in my leadership book *How to Lead & Still Have a Life* is that in order to accomplish *more*, you need to do *less*. The secret is to do more of the right stuff, and let go of everything else. We're better off when we do that. That's a principle for life as well as leadership! In the coming pages you will learn that it's okay to say no. As we simplify life, My Life comes back under my control.

Jesus was a less-is-more person. He kept His objectives simple, yet gave Himself wholeheartedly to the people and projects that truly mattered most. As a result, He accomplished more in a short three years than anyone else has ever accomplished in a whole lifetime. What are the few things worth "stressing out" over? To take back your life, reduce complexity and simplify.

Life is out of control...so let's *recapture it.*

The Monster grows more powerful when I view myself as a

helpless victim. It loves to whisper in my ear, "This is just the way it has to be. Life will always be busy, buried, and behind. Just accept it…and keep running as fast as you can. And while you run, think of all the people you can blame. It's their fault, not yours. Just accept whatever I throw your way."

To take back your life, you must switch from reactive victim to proactive responsibility. If this Life is the one you built, then you can and must accept responsibility. Only you, with God's help, can change It and bring It back under control. Every step of the way, you must refuse to be the victim and begin to live proactively instead of reactively. I'm convinced most of us today live a reactive lifestyle. We let other people determine how we're going to live, and we simply react to all the pressures and voices around us.

> SOCIETY HAS TAUGHT US TO FEEL GUILTY WHEN WE DON'T PLEASE EVERYONE AND DO EVERYTHING.

As Christians, we're called to let Jesus Christ direct and control our life. Here's the problem:

> *We can't surrender to Christ
> that which we do not possess.*

If we are always living reactively, driven by the various demands and agendas of others, then we have little to offer Christ. Taking control requires a plan, and that's one of our topics in the pages ahead. To take back my life, I must become proactive and recapture My Life—so I can give it away! I know this sounds paradoxical. Why would we recapture an out-of-control life only to give it away? The difference rests in *who* your life is surrendered to. Be responsible, be proactive, and the Monster grows weak.

Life is overloaded…so let's *do less.*

The Monster loves more. Make more. Buy more. Do more. And feel guilty if you say no to anyone who wants a piece of you.

After all, they are part of Your Life—and besides, didn't Jesus Himself call you to be the servant of all?

One powerful benefit you'll discover in this book is the permission to say no without feeling guilty. Society has taught us to feel guilty when we don't please everyone and do everything. There comes a time when we need to walk away and just say no. That's not only a slogan for kids being enticed to take drugs; it is a message for the Monster when it comes calling with a long list of demands. No matter what your calling in life, you must learn to say no when you're overloaded.

Jesus knew when to say yes and when to say no. We're going to learn about accomplishing *more* by doing *less* by focusing on that which matters most. We need to do less of *whatever* and more of *what matters.* You've already tried the *more* approach to life, now let's try *less!* Choose to do less, learn to say no, and the Monster will grow weaker by the day.

Life is actually underutilized...
in Christ, we can *accomplish more.*

So far we've emphasized our need to reduce, slow down, simplify, and do less. But there is a surprise just around the bend. As you begin to say, "No thank you, I'm not following It anymore," your New Life becomes *more* productive, not *less.* You discover that your potential for serving God, loving the key people in your life, and moving forward in your career actually increases. You learn that it wasn't so much the size of your dreams that created the Monster, but rather, the path you choose as you chased those dreams. When My Life becomes His Life, surrendered to Christ and lived in His strength by His Spirit, my potential in all aspects of my life goes UP! Parents become better moms and dads. Marriages become sweeter. Work becomes a calling, not a curse.

Life tells me to climb higher on the ladder of success… but true success is not up the ladder, but down!

And there is one more surprise as you begin to tackle My Life and get it under control. The Monster loves to climb. My Life defined success as climbing to the top. Being the best. Being in charge and calling the shots. But the higher we climb, the longer the ladder seems to grow. It's as if it lengthens as we climb. To take back your life, you will need to climb *down* the ladder. Real success and true greatness is found not at the top but at the bottom. Jesus once said to a group of young leaders, "If you want to be great, be a servant" (see Matthew 20:26).

ONE MORE PROMOTION, ONE MORE POSSESSION, ONE MORE VACATION, AND THEN IT WILL LET YOU REST. BUT IT IS NEVER SATISFIED.

The prideful heart of the Monster loves to look down on people, to lead the climb up the ladder, to win the race and capture the prize. And besides, It really believes that real happiness awaits at the top of the climb. The good life is just a few more rungs up but always barely out of reach. One more promotion, one more possession, one more vacation, and then It will let you rest. But It is never satisfied. It must keep climbing.

To take back your life, you must quit climbing higher and harder. Success as our prideful It defines it is an illusion. In the coming chapters, we will learn that real success, real joy, and real life is found by climbing *down* the ladder, not *up*. Now hear me clearly—I'm *not* saying, "Abandon your dreams, settle for mediocrity, and forget ever being promoted." It's not the climbing that's the problem, it's the direction. Our culture tells us to ascend to greatness, but Jesus said we're to descend to greatness. If you want to be great, be a servant. There is nothing wrong with excelling or achieving. God wants us to be good stewards of the gifts and talents He has given to us and develop them to the max. But if you hope to tame an out-of-control life, you'll need to change directions.

Before you read on...begin to choose life.

It's been said, "Insanity is doing the same thing over and over and expecting different results." If you want this year to be better than last year, you must choose a new course. Make a change. You can do it! Most of our life is really a result of the habits we form and live out daily, often without even thinking. These habits are the result of our daily choices, little decisions made moment by moment. To change your life, you must change your habits. And to change your habits, you must change your decisions, one at a time. With the help of Christ, you can do it. You can prayerfully, carefully choose a new direction. Don't put it off! Today is the first day of the rest of your life.

Each chapter of my book concludes with pages designed to encourage you toward making those little changes, those little choices, which work together to change a life. Don't skip them. Better yet, get with a group of friends and process them together. As you do, you will form what I'll later call a "life-team," journeying together to take back life as God designed it to be lived!

TAKE BACK YOUR LIFE!

WARNING:

Pride drives us to climb the ladder of success.

TAKE-BACK TIP #1:

*Stop climbing, for success is not found at the top.
Instead, climb down the ladder to success!*

STOP CLIMBING

Start Down the

Ladder to Success

We live in a driven culture. The Monster called My Life loves to drive—and the faster, the better. It has convinced many of us to push the pedal to the metal and ignore all speed limits. That's why so many of us are living in the fast lane. Some of us are driven to get the checkered flag and finish first. Others of us aren't driven to finish first; we're just trying to keep up with the person ahead while not getting passed by the maniac riding our bumper. We feel trapped, boxed into the fast lane of the freeway with no exit in sight. After all, if everyone else is driving this fast, do we really have a choice?

Sure, we could pull over and quit the race. But who can afford that? The bills have to be paid, and no one wants to be left behind. So we keep accelerating in the hope that we won't get run over.

Years ago, we jumped into the race with a vision of winning and enjoying the good life in the winner's circle. Now the goal has shifted from victory to mere survival. Just make it around the next turn, and enjoy an occasional pit stop along the way. We live for that next long weekend of rest. We drive hard with our sights set on our next vacation, which is just around the bend. These brief stops are fun, but seldom fulfilling. And before we know it, the pit crew pushes us back into the race, whether we are ready or not. So with white knuckles we grasp the wheel, put the pedal to the metal, and resume the insanity.

But does life have to be lived under such intense pressure? Shouldn't it be more like a joyful journey, a challenging yet fulfilling road trip? Shouldn't our daily journey make us better people, move us toward our goals, and allow us to live with a measure of sanity? In short, can we pursue our dreams without having our life become a nightmare? The answer is an undeniable *yes!*

Climbing Down to Move Up

We all want to climb the ladder, move up in life, and achieve some goals that were once only dreams. And there is nothing wrong with a life that aspires to greatness. But living to climb the ladder of success can be frustrating. It seems the higher you go, the longer the ladder gets. The rungs above you, just out of reach, always seem to increase in number. So you climb faster, striving for the top. Yet the top never comes, and you wonder if you're making any progress at all.

I've been there, so I know the feeling. And many of the people I talk to today say, "Dale, my life is too fast, too complex, too out of control. I don't know how much longer I can keep this up." What can we do to restore some sanity to our lives? Do we have to give up on our dreams and goals and settle for mediocrity in order to live a balanced life? Or can we go for it, stay in the race, chase our dreams during the day, and still sleep well at night?

These are the questions I hope to answer in this book. There *is* a better way to climb the ladder, or run the race before you. Jesus Christ is the ultimate role model of a balanced person who also happened to be the most visionary leader in human history.

Jesus was not one to settle for mediocrity. With a handful of followers, He launched a global movement called the church. We're talking a huge goal here. And yet He did not overload His life or stress Himself out as He pursued His dream. Was He successful? Absolutely. Was He great? The greatest man who ever lived. Was He out of control, exhausted, and living for the next weekend? Not at all. He pursued and achieved great things, but He did so by using a radically different approach to greatness.

The Paradoxical Secret to Greatness

The way God defines real success is somewhat of a paradox. It's what I call the *humility paradox*. As we work our way through this book, I believe you'll agree that humility is a key thread that runs through much of what the Bible teaches about pursuing and enjoying real success. What God teaches about greatness is radically different from what our culture declares:

> *God says that to be great, you*
> *must be a servant and climb down*
> *the ladder to success.*

When we view true success from God's perspective, we discover that it's found at the *bottom* of the ladder rather than at the top. The paradox is that you can be at the top of your organization, the best in your profession, and at the bottom of the ladder at the same time! Even more surprising is that climbing *down* actually speeds up your *ascent* to be the best that you can be.

I think, for example, of the interaction between Jesus and Mary and Martha in Luke chapter 10, when Jesus said, "Martha, Martha, you are worried and bothered about so many things" (verse 41). He had to repeat her name because she was complaining, stressed out about being too busy, and wouldn't shut up! Many of us today find ourselves in the same place as Martha. We're doing everything we possibly can to move up to the next rung on the ladder of success. Like Martha, we're "worried and bothered about so many things."

Now, I don't believe Jesus was suggesting to Martha—or to us—that we should just drop out of life, chill out, and not seek to achieve anything. That wasn't His point. He wasn't against excellence or a job well done. Notice carefully what He said in Matthew 20:26:

> *Whoever wishes to* become great *among*
> *you shall be your servant.*

Jesus had nothing against His disciples' desires to be great. He desired the very best for them as well as for us. Anyone who follows Jesus should indeed become a better person, beyond the norm, even great. Jesus desires not just the good life but the great life for His followers. Yet He *is* concerned about our approach to greatness and our definition of success. He surprised, even shocked, His disciples by declaring that the path to authentic greatness is through servanthood—through humility.

WE THINK SUCCESS COMES FROM CLIMBING *UP* THE LADDER, BUT GOD CALLS US TO CLIMB *DOWN*.

Our Lord's words were spoken in the course of a discussion with the disciples about who would have the most important leadership positions in the kingdom. The mother of James and John had approached Jesus and asked if her sons could sit in the seats to the right and left of Christ's throne. The other disciples became upset when they heard about this request and apparently got vocal about it. That's when Jesus stepped in and said, in essence, "Your approach to success is all wrong. Whoever wants to be great must be a servant."

This truth applies to us, too. We think success comes from climbing *up* the ladder, but God calls us to climb *down*. Not to descend into failure, but success. Not to climb down and abandon the pursuit of our goals, but to climb down in order to achieve our goals. Serving with humility is in fact a key ingredient of successful living.

Matthew 20:26 isn't the only place in the Bible where we find true greatness linked to humility. Consider the following passages:

> *Matthew 18:4*—"Whoever then humbles himself as this child, he is the greatest in the kingdom of heaven."
>
> *Matthew 23:11*—"The greatest among you shall be your servant."
>
> *1 Peter 5:5-6*—"You younger men, likewise, be subject to your elders; and all of you, clothe yourselves with humility toward one another, for God is opposed to the proud, but gives grace to the humble. Therefore humble yourselves under the mighty hand of God, that He may exalt you at the proper time."

The Rungs on God's Ladder of Success

In the coming chapters, we will climb together down the ladder to success. Each rung is important. Together they move us toward true greatness. They were modeled by Jesus and provide ten steps—each one a choice. Step-by-step, they enable us to take back our life and live it as it was meant to be lived. Here are the rungs of the ladder, with a brief description of each choice:

Choice #1: Stop Climbing—Start Down the Ladder to Success

> *Humble yourselves under the mighty hand of*
> *God, that He may exalt you at the proper time*
> *(1 Peter 5:6).*

The first step is simply to stop climbing. Stop defining success in life by the world's dictionary. Success is more than getting ahead, owning the most toys, and living the good life at the top of the ladder. You don't have to spend your life climbing. Real success and real life is within your reach, but only as you change direction and take a whole new approach to life. Climb, yes, but start climbing down to success. Once you stop and change directions, there are nine more choices that restore life as it was meant to be lived. Each of these nine represents a strategic step down the ladder to life as it's meant to be. They work together to restore control and empower your potential as a child of God to actually accomplish more, not less, with your life.

Choice #2: Let God Be God—Build the Ultimate Alliance

> *Whoever wishes to save his life will lose it, but whoever loses his life for My sake, he is the one who will save it (Luke 9:24).*

What a paradox—the key to taking back or finding your life is losing it. You have to give up your life to gain it.

Pride says, "Hey Lord, this is my life."
Humility says, "Help Lord, here is my life."

If you really want to possess your life, you must first give it up. To get it, give it away. To find it, lose it. Of course, you need to give it over to the right one—God, who loves you and loves all who your life touches.

Choice #3: Don't Barter with Love, Just Give It Away— Make Love Your Gift and People Your Priority

> *Love your enemies, and do good, and lend, expecting nothing in return; and your reward will be great, and you will be sons of the Most*

High; for He Himself is kind to ungrateful
and evil men....Give, and it will be given to
you (Luke 6:35,38).

Unconditional love, the kind of love God lavishes on us, is a powerful force and a vital part of learning how to live life well. It's not easy to love our enemies and do good to them. But in doing so, we follow our Lord's example, expand our love-ability, and enrich every relationship from the bedroom to the boardroom!

Pride says, "I'll love you if..."
Humility says, "I'll love you regardless..."

Love is the only possession that increases when you give it away. If you feel shortchanged on love, then start giving more of it away!

Choice #4: Serve Your Way to Success—Nurture a Servant Spirit

Whoever wishes to become great among you
shall be your servant (Matthew 20:26).

Thinking and living as a servant is essential to having a great life. It actually helps you to succees, enriching every relationship you have. This is true even in the business world, which has often emphasized that it's necessary to step on others in order to get to the top. But research now shows that servant-style leadership brings far greater success. When you use your power, influence, gifts, and abilities to help others succeed, you move forward! And you'll bring honor to God as you do.

Pride says, "What's in it for me?"
Humility says, "What can I do for you?"

The paradox here is that the fastest way to succeed is to live to make others successful. Always ask, "How can I better serve you?" and success will follow.

Choice #5: Chase a Better Dream—Capture God's Vision for Life

> *I do not regard myself as having laid hold of*
> *it yet; but one thing I do: forgetting what lies*
> *behind and reaching forward to what lies*
> *ahead, I press on toward the goal*
> *(Philippians 3:13-14).*

A compelling vision, a God-given dream, can propel us to move forward and accomplish great goals. Without a clear and compelling dream, we have nothing to motivate us. Where are you going? What is the purpose for pressing onward? What is your goal, and what benefit awaits if you accomplish it? A person with a dream overcomes life's obstacles and keeps moving forward.

Pride says, "Things are good enough as they are."
Humility says, "Lord, what are your dreams for me?"

Our paradox here? The key to finishing well is to remember GINFWMY (God is not finished with me yet). The secret to finishing *well* is to remember, *"Well,* I'm *never* finished!"

Choice #6: Build a Life-Team—Never Tackle Life Alone

> *Two are better than one because they have a good*
> *return for their labor. For if either of them falls, the*
> *one will lift up his companion. But woe to the one*
> *who falls when there is not another to lift him up....*
> *A cord of three strands is not quickly torn apart*
> *(Ecclesiastes 4:9-10,12).*

We're more powerful when we work together. Life is a team sport, not a solo endeavor. That's why it is best to tackle the challenges of life with a few trusted and loyal friends. While it's true you want to be the very best individual God can make you, that cannot be done in isolation. All the different members of the body of Christ are gifted in different ways so they can build up one another.

> *Pride says, "Just go it alone."*
> *Humility says, "Lord, who can go with me?"*

Paradoxically, great individuals approach life as a team endeavor. The world says, "Show no weakness. Do it yourself. Stand on your own two feet." Yet the truth is that greatness is found in great teams, great friends, and great families—not in going it alone.

Choice #7: Play to Your Strengths—Stop Trying to Do It All

> *Through the grace given to me I say to everyone among*
> *you not to think more highly of himself than he ought to*
> *think; but to think so as to have sound judgment,*
> *as God has allotted to each a measure of faith*
> *(Romans 12:3).*

God doesn't expect us to be good at everything. In Romans 12:3, the apostle Paul warns us not to think too highly of ourselves, but to stay humble. Then in the verses that follow he declares that the members of Christ's body "do not have the same function" (verse 4). We're all different, and uniquely designed with both strengths and weaknesses. So specialize—focus on your strengths!

> *Pride says, "I'm God's gift to humanity."*
> *Humility says, "What has God given me*
> *that I can give to humanity?"*

The paradox here is that we accomplish *more* when we focus

down and do *less.* The difference between a stagnant swamp and a powerful river is focus and depth. Don't spread yourself too thin.

Choice #8: Improve Your Flex-ability—Be a Lifelong Learner

No one, after drinking old wine wishes for
new; for he says, "The old is good enough"
(Luke 5:39).

To accept good as "good enough" is a dangerous way to live—that's Jesus' point in Luke 5:39. We need to be careful about becoming too content with things as they are. There ought to be a "sanctified discontentment" in the heart of every Christian—a discontentment that says, "I'm not going to rest on what God has done in me or through me in the past. I want to make myself available for whatever direction He wants to take me in the future." There's always progress to be made in each aspect of our lives as a spouse, parent, Christian, leader, employee, student, and so on. We need to stay flexible and keep growing.

Pride says, "I know my way."
Humility says, "Lord, teach me more."

What's the paradox? School often begins the day you graduate. Past successes can become steps toward failure if we let pride tempt us to settle for good as good enough.

Choice #9: Slow Down and Focus—Do One Thing at a Time

Everyone who competes in the games exercises
self-control in all things. They then do it to receive a
perishable wreath, but we an imperishable.
Therefore I run in such a way, as not without aim
(1 Corinthians 9:25-26).

The less-is-more approach to life knows the power of concentrated effort. Many of us allow ourselves to become distracted in so many different directions that we fail to be effective at any one thing. We try to take on everything that comes our way because we want to please people or satisfy our own egos.

Pride says, "Hurry! You must do it all."
Humility says, "Slow down! Focus on what is important."

We need to learn the paradox that the urgent is seldom important, and the important is seldom urgent.

Choice #10: Nurture Sanctified Stubbornness—Keep the Faith No Matter What

Faith is the assurance of things hoped for, the conviction of things not seen (Hebrews 11:1).

In Christ, we always have hope. His crucifixion and resurrection on our behalf gives us the assurance of salvation and eternal life. We can have absolute confidence in God's present care for us and His future plans for us even though we may not see them clearly. It is this confidence, this assurance, that enables us to persevere and not quit. A strong, growing trust in Christ enables us to never lose hope even when times are tough.

Pride says, "Believe in yourself."
Humility says, "Lord, my trust is in You."

Here, the paradox is that the most *certain* things in life are often the *unseen*. The invisible is an essential part of reality. After all, God says faith, hope, and love are the three foundation blocks of a healthy life.

Starting the Journey

Those are the rungs of the ladder. Each one represents a choice, a decision you can make if you want to take back your life. Start choosing to climb a new direction. But as you do, don't climb alone. Ask Jesus Christ to go with you, to guide you, and help you every step of the way. Without Him, you will stumble and fall as we seek to descend to real life and take back life as it was meant to be.

As we work our way through this book together, my challenge to you is that you don't merely study the ladder. Start climbing toward success! Make these rungs a real part of your life. But beware—climbing down a ladder can be scarier than climbing up. If you've ever been on a tall ladder and looked down only to suddenly become aware of the risks of slipping and falling, you know what I mean. So don't be in a hurry. Don't skip rungs. Take your time on each one. Let God perform His work in you every step of the way. And you'll be on your way to taking back your life. You'll be achieving real success, and enjoying life as it was meant to be.

CHOICE #1: **STOP CLIMBING**

Chapter Summary: Get the Big Idea

From the womb, through grade school, into higher education, and then out into the real world we have traveled. And all along the way, we've been fooled and tricked into thinking that climbing the ladder of success would make us happy. It's time to stop the climb, think about life, and listen to the advice of Jesus: "Love God and love people...stop laying up treasures on earth...to be great, be a servant...follow Me, and I will give you life and life abundant." It's time to stop climbing and start rediscovering life as God designed it to be lived. Have you been headed in the wrong direction?

Questions to Guide Discussion and Your Choices

The following questions will guide you in your personal reflection upon and application of this chapter. They can also be used in a group setting for discussion purposes after reading the chapter. Either way, you will want to take the time to prayerfully ask God to guide you and strengthen you as you begin to make wise choices about the rest of your life.

1. Up to today, what desires or dreams have driven you in life? In other words, how have you defined success?

2. As you reflect back on the introduction and chapter 1, what has changed in your thinking about life and real success?

3. In light of this chapter, take some time to redefine your goals for your life. To put it another way, how do you choose to define *success* for yourself from now on?

4. The chapter overviewed nine more choices that work together to empower you, with God's help, to take back your life. Review and reflect on these nine choices.

    a. Which one or two do you feel would come rather easily for you? What are your strengths as you move forward?

    b. Which one or two present the greatest challenge to you in light of your past approach to life?

TAKE BACK YOUR LIFE!

Choice #1: Stop Climbing
Start Down the Ladder to Success

Choice #2: Let God Be God
Build the Ultimate Alliance

Choice #3: Don't Barter with Love—Give It Away
Make Love Your Gift and People Your Priority

Choice #4: Serve Your Way to Success
Nurture a Servant Spirit

Choice #5: Chase a Better Dream
Capture God's Vision for Life

Choice #6: Build a Life-Team
Never Tackle Life Alone

Choice #7: Play to Your Strengths
Stop Trying to Do It All

Choice #8: Improve Your Flex-ability
Be a Lifelong Learner

Choice #9: Slow Down and Focus
Do One Thing at a Time

Choice #10: Nurture Sanctified Stubbornness
Keep the Faith No Matter What

WARNING:
Pride says, "Hey, Lord, this is my *life."*

TAKE-BACK TIP #2:
Humility says, "Help, Lord
—here is my life.*"*

LET GOD BE GOD

Build the

Ultimate Alliance

In our pursuit of the good life, we often pin our hopes on modern technology, which is supposed to help us save time and be more efficient. But the reality is that our gadgets haven't made life better. Rather, they've made life faster! And with that speed comes greater complexity and more pressure to keep up the pace. In one sense, life may have become a little easier because so much of it is automated. But at the same time, our world is asking and expecting more of us. The Monster is never satisfied!

Life has also become more complicated because we've insisted on more and more choices, and we've gotten them. But again, more choices don't make life better—just busier!

For example, do you remember the days when there were only three major networks to choose from on the television? We were content to click the dial between ABC, NBC, and CBS and enjoy our choice in low-definition black and white. Life was good and simple.

Today, however, when we reach for our remote control, turn on our high-definition, large-screen TV, and begin to surf our options, we are confronted with hundreds of channels with thousands of programs, plus an array of pay-per-view extras including hundreds of movies old and new! Yes, we have more options, but less life. The mere act of trying to decide what to watch so we can relax now stresses us out!

And what about the simple pleasure of a cup of coffee? A few years ago if you were asked, "Would you like a cup of coffee?" that meant a couple of major choices and an off-brand or two. I read recently that there are now over 550 different brands of coffee. In restaurants, the only decision facing us was caffeinated or decaf. Now we go to specialty cafes or kiosks with literally dozens of different choices. My wife's favorite order at Starbucks is a café latte, half-caf, extra hot, extra shot, breve with nonfat vanilla syrup. More coffee, less life. And My Life, driven by the Monster's desire for "the best" of everything, demands that I pay whatever price it takes to have the best. After all, I deserve it as I prepare for my long day at the office!

We also have many more choices when it comes to food. In 1978, the average grocery store carried about 11,000 products. Today, it's about 30,000 and climbing. The only reason that number isn't higher is because the stores are running out of shelf space.

Making matters worse is the fact that we not only have more choices, but we also insist that those choices be available to us *right now*. We live in a high-speed, I-want-it-now culture. Tim Kimmel, in his book *Little House on the Freeway*, describes the American family in this way:

> The first pressure that comes from a society that values being hurried [is] we have grown accustomed to having everything NOW. We are the instant generation. We like to tell a sign behind a restaurant what we'd like for dinner and then expect them to be holding it out

the window by the time we pull our car around to the drive-thru.[1]

Isn't that true? Tim goes on:

> We cut projects down to the wire because we know that we can ship a package anywhere in the continental United States (and now abroad) within twenty-four hours. Automatic teller machines now give us instant cash. Microwave ovens give us immediate meals. Malls give us sudden debt.
>
> We have a love affair with haste. We call it convenience and there is no doubt that many of our modern conveniences have made some of the mundane duties of life more tolerable. But there is a subtle programming that goes on at the same time. It's not long before we drive our lives the way we drive our cars—too fast.[2]

When you consider the fast pace of our lives and the complexity of our choices, it's no wonder we're getting so stressed out. Now there's nothing wrong with technology, speed, or choices. Like most Americans, I'll pay more for all three! The real problem is the stress that comes with the lifestyle that is robbing us of life as it's meant to be. We are missing the life Jesus wants us to experience as Christians. Notice what He says about the kind of relationship we can enjoy with Him:

> *Come to Me, all who are weary and heavy-laden, and I will give you rest. Take My yoke upon you and learn from Me, for I am gentle and humble in heart, and you will find rest for your souls. For My yoke is easy and My burden is light (Matthew 11:28-30).*

For most of us "easy" and "light" don't define our lives. And did you notice Jesus said He is "humble in heart"? That humility factor keeps popping up. However, Christ is not setting an unattainable standard when He speaks of lightening the load we carry. He means it when He promises rest.

That's a great promise from Jesus—rest! As we work our way through this book, we're going to walk with Jesus and let Him teach us how to rest—how to make our burden easier and our load lighter. We're going to discover that we really can reduce the complexity of life and slow it down a bit without dropping out or shutting ourselves up in a monastery. We will learn a better way to pursue great dreams without having our personal life turn into a nightmare.

To start, we need to recognize that all of life flows from the inside out. It starts in the heart, and moves outward from there. We find this confirmed in Proverbs 4:23: "Watch over your heart with all diligence, for from it flow the springs of life." In other words, life is lived at the heart level before it reaches the mouth, hands, or feet. There are issues of the heart that will either make us or break us as we try to live life God's way and take back our lives. And at the root of those heart issues is the problem of pride. The fast-climbing, always-driven, never-content Monster in our lives is driven by pride.

The Problem of Pride

It's amazing how pride comes to us so naturally. It's our pride that says, "This is *my* life, God...leave me alone. I'm in charge; I'm old enough to take care of myself." In essence, pride prevents us from surrendering our life to God and partnering with Him as we live it. Our prideful attempts to preserve our own nearsighted vision of how life should be lived keeps the balanced life Jesus intended for us as a blurry, unattainable shadow in the background.

Pride says, "Hey, Lord, this is my *life."*

The Effects of Pride

Here are three points we need to understand about pride and its harmful effect on our lives:

1. *Pride drives us*

Pride, which is part of our fallen human nature, drives us to climb the ladder of success and to do so as fast as we can. If you view yourself more highly than you ought, then of course you will think you deserve more than you have been given. Consequently, you will strive for what you believe you deserve. "More" no longer is a blessing but a right, and thus you feel driven to climb regardless of the cost.

2. *Pride is never satisfied*

With each new rung of the ladder comes a vision of several more. By the time we reach a goal, it no longer has its original allure and we're driven to go even higher. Luxuries that were once dreams, after we've obtained them, no longer fulfill us. For example, a cell phone was once a luxury for the rich and famous; now they are a necessity for every junior high student! And on top of that, a *real* phone should double as our MP3 player, carry around our entire music collection, take pictures, and connect to the World Wide Web! No matter what we achieve or obtain, we soon become enticed by the next generation of technology or innovation.

> PRIDE BLINDS US TO THE FACT THAT THE WORLD CAN NEVER DELIVER ON ITS PROMISES.

The reality is, what we have now is *never* enough. It's as if the gadgets of the world were like a drug. You indulge, it feels good for a while, but once the newness wears off, you need a higher dose of the drug to get the same happiness or kick that you got before. Pride has a way of continually extending the ladder of success with a spirit of discontentment.

3. *Pride blinds us*

Pride blinds us to the fact that the world can never deliver on its promises. King Solomon is a good example of this. If ever a man had everything he could have wanted, it was Solomon. He had incalculable wealth, a vast array of women, and the power and prestige of a king. From the world's perspective, he lacked nothing. In fact, in Ecclesiastes 2:10 he said, "All that my eyes desired I did not refuse them. I did not withhold my heart from any pleasure, for my heart was pleased because of all my labor and this was my reward for all my labor." Not only did Solomon allow himself everything, through his pride he perceived himself as deserving of everything because of his labor. The Monster whispered to him, "You deserve it all," and he believed it.

Even though Solomon had everything he wanted, he still came to this rather stunning conclusion: "I considered all my activities which my hands had done and the labor which I had exerted, and behold all was vanity and striving after the wind and there was no profit under the sun" (Ecclesiastes 2:11). Solomon had it all...yet it gave him nothing. The riches of the world failed to deliver on their promises.

That's why 1 John 2:15-16 warns,

> *Do not love the world nor the things in the world. If anyone loves the world, the love of the Father is not in him. For all that is in the world, the lust of the flesh and the lust of the eyes and the boastful pride of life, is not from the Father, but is from the world.*

Did you notice what the passage says about the "boastful pride of life"? It's not from the Father. And neither are the other two rungs that are found on the world's ladder to success—the "lust of the flesh" (sensuality) and the "lust of the eyes" (materialism).

John then declares, "The world is passing away, and also its lusts; but the one who does the will of God lives forever" (verse

17). It's interesting to note John's choice of words. He doesn't chastise us for enjoying the things of this world. Rather, he warns us not to fall in *love* with them, not to *lust* after them. He's warning us not to make them our gods.

Instead of chasing these temporary pleasures, we can choose to pursue the will of God—to let God be God! We can live a different lifestyle, chase a different kind of dream. This lifestyle includes a different kind of abundance—an abundance in Christ. Jesus said, "I came that [you] may have life, and have it abundantly" (John 10:10).

The Antidote to Pride

Pride can never be managed on our own. We need help. In my book *How to Lead & Still Have a Life*, I wrote this about the importance of one's spiritual life in today's hectic world:

> The leader whose spiritual life is weak and ill-defined will find himself at the mercy of his world—a world that can never quite make up its mind what it wants. A world that cares not for the life of the leader, but only for what it can extract from him. It is a hungry world whose appetite is insatiable and whose demands can never be totally fulfilled.[3]

It is a danger faced by every leader and follower, employer and employee, young and old. One day we're told to be one kind of person, then before you know it, society changes its mind. We have competing demands and expectations placed upon us because trends are always changing. So we end up confused and unfulfilled as we chase the latest fad or opinion poll. We climb higher only to be told, that's not high enough—keep climbing!

If you want to avoid being a casualty of such a world, you need to anchor your life upon strong convictions that come from an authentic spirituality at the core of your life. That's why life balance begins with our relationship with God. And we can't limit our time with God to Sundays; we must learn to draw upon Him 24/7. Not until we let God be God and Lord of our lives can we begin to disarm the Monster and take back our life.

The Losses from Pride

Pride promises great gain but actually delivers real loss. In Luke 9:24-25, Jesus said, "Whoever wishes to save his life will lose it, but whoever loses his life for My sake, he is the one who will save it. For what is a man profited if he gains the whole world, and loses or forfeits himself?"

There are at least three significant losses that result from following these little gods of our culture and not letting God truly be the God of our lives.

You Can Lose Your Soul

Jesus speaks in hyperbole in Luke 9:24-25 to make a point: Even if you become the owner of the entire planet, you still lose in the end if you forfeit your soul for eternity. The reality is that the pursuits of the world can be such a strong distraction in our life that we never take the time to consider our spiritual life or our need for a Savior. When we're a self-made person, we're far less likely to see our need for the salvation of our soul. Instead, we buy into the idea that we can save ourselves or that this life on planet Earth is all that really matters.

You Can Lose Eternal Rewards

Even if you are a Christian headed for heaven by God's grace and faith in Christ alone, you can still lose the rewards waiting for you in heaven. I'm not talking about losing your salvation, but your eternal rewards. When your whole life is invested in this world and following its little gods, you've got nothing left to invest in eternity. Jesus tries to redirect our life-stock to a sounder and more worthwhile investment by exhorting us to "store up for [ourselves] treasures in heaven, where neither moth nor rust destroys, and where thieves do not break in or steal" (Matthew 6:20). Where are you investing yourself? In the things of earth, which one day will disappear, or the things of heaven? The treasures you store up in heaven will be yours for all eternity, but the stuff of this world stays behind. The Monster whispers, "Live for today," but God wisely counsels us to invest in eternity. Matthew 6:20 reminds us that real success is not at the top of the world's ladder, but at the bottom of the cross with Christ.

You Can Miss the Joy of Abundant Life in Christ

The joy of the Christian life can start right now. Storing up treasures in heaven is an eternal investment, but eternity begins right now! We don't have to wait till heaven for a return on our investment. We can experience joy right now here on earth. Life will always have its challenges and pains, and we will suffer at times because we live on a fallen planet populated by fallen people. But Jesus clearly promised, "I came that they may have life, and have it abundantly" (John 10:10). So what do you have to lose? Nothing at all! Life *now* and in *eternity* is best lived surrendered to the will and wisdom of God.

Shifting from Pride to Humility

So where do we go from here? How do we get started down the ladder to real success? It begins by humbling ourselves and surrendering ourselves to Christ—and not as a one-time event, but as an everyday discipline.

> *Humility says, "Help, Lord—*
> *here is my life."*

Pride says, "Hey Lord, this is *my* life. I want to live it *my* way." By contrast, humility says, "Help, Lord, *here* is my life. I offer it to You. I can't do it without You." This is what Christ meant when He said, "If anyone wishes to come after Me, he must deny himself, and take up his cross daily and follow Me. For whoever wishes to save his life will lose it, but whoever loses his life for My sake, he is the one who will save it" (Luke 9:23-24).

Notice the key words here:

- "come *after Me*"

- "*deny* himself"

- "*take up* his cross daily"

- "follow *Me*"

- "loses his life for *My sake*"

What do those key words tell us? That the Christian life is one of letting God be God, that the Lord of creation deserves to be the Lord of my life. To take back my life, I must first surrender it to my Lord Jesus Christ. I must choose to follow Him instead of this Life of my own creation. We can't live such a life and climb up the ladder to worldly success at the same time. They oppose each other by nature. The world's approach to life, rooted in pride, lives on the premise of *take* in order to *receive*. The real Christian life, rooted in humility, lives on the premise of *give* and you will *receive*.

> WE MUST BE CONTENT TO LIVE IN THE SHADOW OF GOD.

Now at first glance, the surrendered life does not appear as such a glamorous alternative to all that the world dangles before us. So what is so wonderful about experiencing a life surrendered to God? Let's take a look at what the surrendered life looks like when put into practice.

The Surrendered Life—God's Design from Start to Finish

God intended for us to live surrendered from the very beginning of time. In Genesis 1:26 God said, "Let Us make man in Our image, according to Our likeness." Verse 27 goes on to say, "God created man in His own image, in the image of God He created him; male and female He created them." Already we see that God created us to live in His shadow—a humble position. Then Genesis 3:8 states that Adam and Eve "heard the sound of the LORD God walking in the garden in the cool of the day." In other words, from the very beginning, even before we fell into sin, we were designed to walk and live contently in that humble relationship of submission to God. We must be content to live in the shadow of God, understanding that He is the big deal in the universe. We are, as the psalmist says, "the sheep of His pasture" (Psalm 100:3). And that's okay. The world will see this as a sign of weakness, when in reality it is a sign of real wisdom. Just as a fish is wise, not weak, in acknowledging its need for water, so we are at our best when we see our need to live in submission to God.

John the Baptist got it. Although specially gifted by God and popular among the masses, he was content to redirect attention to Jesus. In fact, it fulfilled him to do so. He did not allow his God-given success to result in personal pride. Rather, John pointed his listeners to Jesus, insisting, "He must increase, but I must decrease" (John 3:30). He recognized himself as a mere man, made in the image of God. While others wanted to idolize him, he redirected their attention to the real star of the show, Jesus the Messiah and Savior of all mankind.

Not only is it God's design for us to live in humble relationship to Him here on earth, but it is also His plan for all eternity. Revelation 21:3 says, "The tabernacle of God is among men, and He will dwell among them, and they shall be His people, and God Himself will be among them." In heaven, one of our chief occupations will be to worship and glorify God forever, which requires humility on our part. Once we see Him face to face, it will come easy. But for now, it takes a regular discipline of worship to remind us that it's not about us; it's all about Him!

Surrender Is Central to the First Commandment

In Exodus 20:2-3, God proclaimed, "I am the LORD your God, who brought you out of the land of Egypt, out of the house of slavery. You shall have no other gods before Me." Here, God clearly states where we stand in relation to Him. We're to remain humble before Him. After all, in the first half of this passage He reminds us of our need for and dependence upon Him. In the second half He commands us to put Him first in our lives with "no other gods before [Him]," and that means not even ourselves. Yet pride encourages us to deify ourselves.

Surrender Is at the Heart of the Great Commandment

Jesus said, "You shall love the Lord your God with all your heart, and with all your soul, and with all your mind. This is the great and foremost commandment" (Matthew 22:37-38). This command requires complete surrender on our part. Let's look more closely at what this would look like in our life.

The Surrendered Life Is Motivated by Grace and Maintained by Love

We as Christians sometimes fall into a mind-set in which we think we must do certain things or act certain ways in order to earn God's love and acceptance. In other words, we submit to God and obey Him because we want desperately to earn His favor. But that's not what God desires. God yearns for His grace to draw us to want to follow Him. He wants our obedience to come not from a sense of forced duty, but from a heart overflowing with love and gratitude. He wants our life to be motivated by grace and maintained by love.

From the garden of Eden to today, God has always given those created in His image a choice. He could have forced us into loving and obeying Him, but He didn't. Rather, He gave us the freedom to either follow Him or flee from Him, to love Him or hate Him. By allowing us this choice, He also created an opportunity to bless us for making the right choice. This freedom of choice, though dangerous and at times destructive, is essential to authentic love.

Jesus put it this way in John 14:23: "If anyone loves Me, he will keep My word; and My Father will love him, and We will come to him and make Our abode with him." He wants us to surrender to Him not because we *have to*, but because we *want to*. He desires a submission and humility that originates from and facilitates an ever-deepening love relationship with Jesus Christ.

The Surrendered Life Allows God to Empower, Enrich, and Guide Us

When we talk about surrender, it may sound like we're talking about a loss or a giving up of something. And it's true that when you surrender your life to God, you are offering control of it to Christ as Lord. However, this surrender does not leave you with loss or emptiness. Rather, it allows God the opportunity to give you back your life and help you live it as it's meant to be lived. There is tremendous blessing in such surrender.

God gives us the strength to do what we need to do. He wants to enrich our life, not take from it. He wants to make our life more abundant and guide us. But He won't force His blessings upon us. Rather, He waits for us to surrender in humility and ask Him for His help. In doing so, we make room for God in our life. That is why Jesus said, "He who loses his life for My sake will find it."

Jesus said, "Abide in Me, and I in you. As the branch cannot bear fruit of itself unless it abides in the vine....I am the vine, you are the branches; he who abides in Me and I in him, he bears much fruit, for apart from Me you can do nothing" (John 15:4-5). What a great reminder! If we're trying to live our life without first surrendering to Christ and letting Him be our source of power and guidance, then we're wasting our time and energy. If we are constantly gorging ourselves on the nutritionless successes of the world, we will never have an appetite for the bread of life—the written and living Word of God. We have to empty ourselves to make room for God to fill us up and give us the life we so desire.

Taking the First Steps

So how do you begin this descent down the ladder to God's kind of success? How do you begin to let God be God in your life? Start choosing...

In Humility, Choose Christ as Your Savior

You may have already surrendered your life to Christ and begun your descent, but in case you have not, do not miss this essential first step. You might be like Nicodemus, a devout Jewish religious leader who recognized that Jesus had come from God. Yet Nicodemus realized that, in spite of his religious stature and many accomplishments, something was still missing in his life. He was even a fan of Jesus. Yet he needed life—not just physical life, but spiritual. That's why Jesus told Nicodemus, "You must be born again" (John 3:7). In essence our Lord was saying, "You are dead within, and you need to believe in Me and live!" It was this encounter that led to some of Jesus' most famous words and to the best-known verse in Scripture: "God so loved the world, that He gave His only begotten Son, that whoever believes in Him shall not perish, but have eternal life" (John 3:16).

> WE HAVE TO EMPTY OURSELVES TO MAKE ROOM FOR GOD TO FILL US UP.

To come to Christ means to recognize you are a sinner in need of forgiveness, and that you are climbing the wrong ladder! Scripture actually says that we are enemies of God, living at enmity with Him (Romans 5:10). Now you may not feel like an enemy of God's, but by denying Him His rightful place as Lord of your life, you are placing yourself as king of your little "kingdom." You need to let God be God and trust in Christ. This means believing that He alone can save you, pay the penalty for your sins, and give you eternal life. All of this, of course, is a choice that calls for true humility. This first and most important act of humility is necessary before you can continue your journey down the ladder to success.

If this is your need, stop right now and pray along these lines:

Father God, thank You for sending Jesus Christ, Your Son, to die on the cross for my sins. I see now my need for a Savior and friend such as Christ. I cannot do it alone. I humbly place my trust and faith in Christ and ask Him into my life. It is out of control and I need His help as I seek to take back my life. As a first step in that direction, I give You my life. Lead me and I will follow. Enable me and I will trust in Your Spirit. Thank You for Your grace in giving me new life in Christ. In Jesus' name I pray. Amen.

(If you prayed that prayer and would like a free CD on growing in Christ, e-mail me by going to www.daleburke.com and let me know of your decision. I'd love to hear from you and help you grow!)

With Humility, Choose Daily to Follow Christ as Lord

If one faction involved in a war surrenders one day and then takes up arms the next, the battle will continue despite the pronounced surrender. Therefore, surrender requires daily ongoing submission. Remember, Luke 9:23 says we need to take up our cross "daily" and follow Christ. Why daily? Maybe it is because we feel so comfortable being in control of our own lives. We've been learning to take control since birth! Giving up that control feels unnatural, even scary at times. Pride tempts us daily and whispers, "It's your life to live." And yet we should never be afraid to yield ourselves completely to Christ. Here are four good reasons to let God be God:

- *Christ loves you deeply.* He proved it when He died on the cross for you. If anyone deserves to be entrusted with your life, it is the One who gave up His life for you.

- *Christ promises His presence and power as we follow Him.* Christ's demands, while they always stretch us, are achievable. He knows us better than anyone else. He knows what we can and cannot handle. He will never allow us to be tempted beyond what we can bear or end up in a circumstance we cannot endure. He may stretch us, but He will never break us. His Spirit enables us to succeed.

• *Christ's resources are sufficient.* The apostle Paul said, "My God will supply all your needs" (Philippians 4:19). God won't always give us all that we *want*, but He promises to always give us all that we *need.* Count on it!

• *Christ sees the big picture and the long-term view of your life.* He knows what is best for you and for His kingdom. He sees the ramifications of every decision for all of eternity. He sees the global impact of your life, crafted by Him, for all time. And He understands you better than you understand yourself. So trust Him and humbly yield to Him in all that you do. He is worthy of our complete trust.

So there you have it. It's tough to give up control of our life, but life gets much tougher when we don't. We struggle because we think we can direct our life better than God can.

I believe God loves us and is able to guide and direct us by His Spirit, who lives in His followers. But today's world is the busiest and noisiest in human history. If you hope to hear from God—to be prompted, directed, or advised by Him—you'll need to set aside a time a place to connect. To get started, review the suggestions in the sidebar on page 50 entitled "Listening for God's Voice" (excerpted from my book *How to Lead & Still Have a Life* [Eugene, OR: Harvest House Publishers, 2004], p. 61). Though you may not literally hear His voice, I believe you will get His message.

But we have a Lord who loves us, is realistic, is sufficient, and is all-knowing. While we may appear to be losing something by surrendering everything, in actuality, we're now positioned to receive the gifts of life from the hand of our heavenly Father. By humbling ourselves, we are going back to God's original design from the beginning of creation. Don't you want to put Him at the center of your life and live the way He intended for you to live? If so, then humble yourself before Him and start climbing down!

Listening for God's Voice

- *Daily Time with God.* Develop the discipline of meeting with God daily. Open His Word and read, reflecting on its truths and principles. Read with a prayerful attitude, asking God to show you what you need to learn today. God often speaks when you are quiet and alone with Him in prayer and reading His Word.

- *Memorize His Word.* Find key verses in God's Word and commit them to memory. Meditate on them. If this sounds intimidating, simply start by writing key verses on life and leadership on small "business cards" and carry one in your pocket at all times. Read it several times a day. Before long, you will have it memorized. God often speaks to us by bringing His Word to mind as we make decisions.

- *Weekly Time in Worship.* Maintain a weekly time of worship. Don't just "go to church," but go with the expectation that God will remind you of who He is, what He has done for you, and the beauty of His love relationship with you as your heavenly Father. God often speaks as you focus on Him in worship.

- *A Group of Like-Minded Friends.* Meet regularly, either weekly or monthly, with a group of peers who share your faith and commitment to integrating God's values into every segment of life, especially your work. Ideally, find others who are in the same or similar occupations, or others who can help you process better the demands you face every day as a leader. God often speaks through friends who also have a relationship with Him.

- *Monthly Refocus Time.* Some leaders find it helpful to set aside a half a day each month, or even a full day, to be alone and review life. Pray as you reflect on your priorities and review your key objectives. Then ask God to guide you as you adjust for the coming month. God often speaks when you slow down and review what matters most.

- *Annual Retreats.* At least once a year, get away for a few days of rest, reflection, and relaxation with God. Use this time to reevaluate and refocus your life and leadership. Read God's Word and just think about your life. Ask God to bring to mind ideas for refining your priorities or plans. God often often speaks when we get away from the noise of everyday life and think, alone, with Him.

CHOICE #2: **LET GOD BE GOD**

Chapter Summary: Get the Big Idea
God is infinitely wise, loves you with a passion, and sees all of your life in a snapshot. Jesus referred to Himself as the Good Shepherd who would die for His sheep. So doesn't it make sense to trust Him, follow Him, and choose His plan for your life? After all, you're not God. Choose today to begin to let God be God—daily, completely, and with no regret. And when you forget or rebel or just simply choose to do it your way, be honest, confess it to Him, and thank Him for His sweet forgiveness, love, and grace.

Questions to Guide Discussion and Your Choices
1. Since the beginning of time, men and women have allowed pride to convince them to say, "This is my life," or "I'll do it my way." Reflect on your choices and ask yourself, "Where is my pride working against me?"

2. Pride often leads us to live overstressed lives. Is your life currently out of balance, and, if so, how would you like it to change?

3. Jesus said, "To find life, you must first lose it; to get it, you must give it up." What does this paradox mean to you and your life?

4. God calls us to surrender our life to Him. What are the benefits to such a radical move? What appealed to you as you read about the benefits of giving up your life?

5. Toward the end of the chapter we discovered four great facts about Jesus Christ. How do these truths affect your decision to let God be God and relax under His direction?

6. Review the page "Listening for God's Voice." What is your plan for creating times of solitude, times alone with God, and time in His Word? In the coming months, try all six of the disciplines listed on that page.

TAKE BACK YOUR LIFE!

Choice #1: Stop Climbing
Start Down the Ladder to Success

Choice #2: Let God Be God
Build the Ultimate Alliance

Choice #3: Don't Barter with Love—Give It Away
Make Love Your Gift and People Your Priority

Choice #4: Serve Your Way to Success
Nurture a Servant Spirit

Choice #5: Chase a Better Dream
Capture God's Vision for Life

Choice #6: Build a Life-Team
Never Tackle Life Alone

Choice #7: Play to Your Strengths
Stop Trying to Do It All

Choice #8: Improve Your Flex-ability
Be a Lifelong Learner

Choice #9: Slow Down and Focus
Do One Thing at a Time

Choice #10: Nurture Sanctified Stubbornness
Keep the Faith No Matter What

WARNING:
Pride says, "I'll love you if...."

TAKE-BACK TIP #3:
Humility says, "I'll love you regardless...."

DON'T BARTER WITH LOVE—GIVE IT AWAY

Make Love Your Gift

and People Your Priority

The Bible is a big book. It was written over the course of centuries, and it includes many hundreds of accounts of what happened to multitudes of people and nations through the ages. Along the way, there are thousands of inspired truths related to God's plan for redeeming humanity and restoring life as it was meant to be. We find all this documented on many hundreds of pages of text. My personal Bible contains 1,033 pages of double-column, small-print passages of holy Scripture!

All that to say, the Bible contains a lot of information.

But did you know it's possible for us to pick out just *one* truth—one statement—that encompasses all of what we find in the Bible? It can be done; in fact, Jesus Himself did it. So if you're looking for one key truth that can help you take back your life and recapture life as it was meant to be, this is it.

In Matthew 22, a lawyer asked Jesus the question, "Teacher, which is the great commandment in the Law?" (verse 36). In other words, what's the big idea? And Jesus responded,

"You shall love the Lord your God with all your heart, and
with all your soul, and with all your mind."
This is the great and foremost commandment.
The second is like it, "You shall love your neighbor as yourself."
On these two commandments depend the whole
Law and the Prophets (verses 37-39).

What Jesus was saying is that you can take all of God's wisdom for life, and, at its core, come to just one key word: love. Love God, and love people. Make this your priority. The apostle Paul builds on this later when he says, "Now faith, hope, love, abide these three; but the greatest of these is love" (1 Corinthians 13:13).

LOVE GOD, AND LOVE PEOPLE. MAKE THIS YOUR PRIORITY.

Once we stop climbing and get God's perspective on success, we begin to take back our life by nurturing our love relationship with God. We build that "ultimate alliance" and let God be God. But don't overlook the second half of this great commandment: Love one another. So if you want to master life, learn to love like Jesus. I'm not kidding. It can be done, but only with some divine assistance. Learning to excel at love empowers life at every level because life is built on relationships. Love well, live well.

What's unfortunate is that the world has attached a lot of baggage to the word *love*. When you talk about love, immediately people think about romance, marriage, or any favorite passion in their lives. We *love* anything and everything from our spouse and kids to our favorite movie, family pet, hometown baseball team (when they are winning) or pepperoni pizza. So what do we really mean by *love*?

And we usually think of love in conditional terms—that is, we feel love for and return love to those who are lovely or who love us first. Or if we lead out with love, we do so to get love in return. I call it *bartering* with love. In a nutshell, our culture trains us to use love as a wage or a bribe:

> *We love as* a bribe *to get what we want. Or we love as* a wage *to pay back what we owe.*

Most of us have perfected the art of bartering with love. It's what we grew up experiencing. Many say it's just the way life works. But that's not the kind of love Jesus was challenging His followers to exhibit. And bartering with love ends up robbing you of life as God intends it to be lived. It puts you under pressure to always be keeping score and balancing your credits and debits as you seek to manipulate the "love market" to your advantage. That is an exhausting game to play!

To take back your life, you've got to learn a new way to love. The secret is learning to love not as a wage or a bribe, but as a *gift*—offered freely with no strings attached. Let's take a closer look at this radical new way of loving.

The Priority of Love

That loving God and loving your neighbor are the greatest commandments makes them the two highest priorities in the Christian life. If we aren't loving God and those around us, then we're missing out on our primary callings.

Now, what exactly is love? For a clear understanding, we must look to the Bible rather than culture. The best passage ever written on God's kind of love is 1 Corinthians 13. There, the apostle Paul talks at length about what true love looks like, how it behaves, and how it relates to others in the real world. This classic passage on love begins by affirming how vital love is to life as it's meant to be.

Unlimited Ability, Without Love, Is Worthless

Paul begins by saying, "If I speak with the tongues of men

and angels, but do not have love, I have become a noisy gong or a clanging cymbal" (verse 1). So even if you could speak every language in the world—including the language of angels—if your words aren't spoken in love, then you're just making noise. Now it's obvious that no one can speak all the languages in the world as well as the language of angels. Paul is using what's known as *hyperbole*—exaggeration used for the purpose of driving home an important point. And the point is this: No matter how wonderful your words, without love, those words mean nothing. So if you think you can talk your way into a balanced life, think again. If you think you can negotiate your way into a better life, give it up. Although better communication may help, great lives are built on great love relationships.

GOD IS NOT PLEASED BY GREAT FAITH WHEN IT'S NOT ACCOMPANIED BY GRACIOUS LOVE.

Unlimited Knowledge, Without Love, Is Useless

Verse 2 continues, "If I have the gift of prophecy, and know all mysteries and all knowledge; and if I have all faith, so as to remove mountains, but do not have love, I am nothing." Again, Paul exaggerates to drive home the point. You could be the most brilliant person on earth, but without love, your vast knowledge is useless. So if you want to take back your life, then learn a new way to love.

Unlimited Faith, Without Love, Is of No Value

Paul then takes us to the spiritual realm: "If I have all faith, so as to remove mountains, but do not have love, I am nothing" (verse 2). You could have incredible faith—the kind that can pray and move mountains—but without love, it would be worthless. God is not pleased by great faith when it's not accompanied by gracious love. So if you think you can go fix your life just by nurturing more faith, you're wrong. I know some people with tremendous faith who still lead messed up, out-of-balance lives. It is possible to be a strong spiritual leader yet not even be nice! Scripture calls us to be great lovers of God and of those around us.

Unlimited Sacrifice, Without Love, Still Disappoints God

Paul concludes his hyperbolic points by saying: "If I give all my possessions to feed the poor, and if I surrender my body to be burned, but do not have love, it profits me nothing" (verse 3). So even the ultimate sacrifice—giving up everything you own and being put to death for your faith—is meaningless if it's not done from love. Such sacrifice doesn't please God; rather, it disappoints Him. So if you think that radical Christian service or sacrifice is the secret to life, wrong again. God loves radical sacrifices, but only when they are accompanied by radical love. It's love that makes life work.

If we want to be successful as Christians, we must increase our "love-ability." We must move beyond bartering with love, which cheapens love and harms our loved ones. Loving as a gift, in the same way God loves us in Christ, must take priority. Without love, we cannot continue climbing down the ladder to God's kind of success.

The Profile of Love

So it's pretty clear that love is vital to life. But what exactly does this kind of love look like? As I mentioned earlier, love is all too frequently misunderstood these days. God is the one who created love, so if we want to know what true love is all about, it makes sense for us to listen to His definition—and He has set it out clearly in 1 Corinthians 13:4-8. Let's look at the passage and break down the essence of love in everyday life:

> *Love is patient, love is kind and not jealous;*
> *love does not brag and is not arrogant, does*
> *not act unbecomingly; it does not seek its own,*

is not provoked, does not take into account a
wrong suffered, does not rejoice in unrigh-
teousness, but rejoices with the truth; bears
all things, believes all things, hopes all things,
endures all things. Love never fails.

Love Is Patient

This means *love waits with contentment.* You communicate love to another person when you wait on him or her without getting frustrated or angry. Merely waiting for someone isn't enough. If you're impatient, or pushy, then you're not being loving. To wait with patience may mean waiting even when it hurts!

Are you patient with your spouse? Your children? Your co-workers? Your friends? How about when you're a customer in a store? Are you patient with those who are serving you? Love is patient. It says to the other person, "You are worth the wait."

Love Is Kind

In short, *love sees a need and meets it.* If you see someone in need and ignore him or her, you're not being kind—and more importantly, you're not being loving. Kindness can take many different forms, but at its root is the simple act of seeing a need and doing something to meet it. It doesn't just feel sorry for the person; it moves with action. That's what love does. This expression of love is most powerful when it comes as a complete surprise. I like to call it "mugging one another" with love. A mugging is a "swift and unexpected act" of violence. Kindness is like mugging someone with love!

Love Is Not Jealous

Love trusts rather than controls. When you're not jealous of someone, it shows you trust that person. You're not suspicious, and you see no need to control that person. Love doesn't hold on to others tightly; rather, it releases them. When you give freedom to others and make them feel trusted, you are on the road to better and healthier relationships.

Love Does Not Brag

In short, *love speaks of others more than one's self.* Consider your conversations. Do you talk more about yourself, or do you ask other people about what's happening in their lives? Do you dominate conversations, or do you ask questions and really listen to the other person? Do you look for opportunities to brag about yourself, or are you quick to praise others at home or at work? Try to openly praise others, and see what happens in your life!

Love Is Not Arrogant

Love exhibits humility, not pride. Love is other-centered, not self-centered. Do you look for opportunities to draw attention to yourself, or do you make an effort to lift up others? The fact love is humble fits in with the humility paradox we've talked about in this book. Remember, the drive to climb up the ladder of success is based in pride. It's all about me; life is centered on me. By contrast, the climb down the ladder toward real success requires humility. Pride short-circuits love, but humility overpowers it!

> A SERVANT SPIRIT IS A POWERFUL TOOL FOR LIFE AS GOD DESIGNED IT TO BE LIVED.

Love Does Not Act Unbecomingly

Love has good manners. That means saying words such as *please* and *thank you.* It means putting other people first and helping them out. When you treat people with respect through good manners, you are loving them. You show appreciation when you express thanks; you show respect when you say, "Please"; you give honor when you open the door and invite others in ahead of you.

Love Does Not Seek Its Own

Love has a servant spirit. In Philippians 2:3-4 Paul wrote, "Do nothing from selfishness or empty conceit, but with humility of mind regard one another as more important than yourselves; do not merely look out for your own personal interests, but also for the interests of others." In Romans 12:10 he wrote, "Be devoted to one another in brotherly love; give preference to one another in honor." So, godly love focuses outward rather than inward. In the next chapter we will explore the power of humility and servant-hood in depth. A servant spirit is a powerful tool for life as God designed it to be lived. The paradox is that to take back your life, you must learn to give it away. More on this mystery later!

Love Is Not Easily Provoked

Another way of saying this is that *love has a slow fuse*. When someone provokes you to anger, do you have a fast fuse or a slow one? Do you lash out, or can you keep your composure? Love keeps the emotions under control, not out of control with rage. Love feels hurt and even anger when it is wronged. There is nothing sinful about feeling angry when you are wronged or wounded by others. Even God feels anger. But the Scriptures caution us with this warning: "Be angry, and yet do not sin, do not let the sun go down on your anger, and do not give the devil an opportunity" (Ephesians 4:26-27). Love handles anger with self-control.

Love Does Not Take into Account a Wrong Suffered

Because we live in a fallen world surrounded by fallen human beings, we're guaranteed of getting hurt by others. People hurt people. Expect it. And Paul says our response should be that of not taking into account a wrong suffered. In other words, love chooses to forgive quickly. Love opts to not keep records of other people's offenses against you. *Love forgives and moves on*. We all have a long list of past wounds and offenses. If you want to move on and take back your life, forgiveness is essential. It frees you to focus on the future and not live in the past. Love allows you to pray, "Lord, You settle my scores for me. I no longer need to get even. Let's move on."

Love Does Not Rejoice in Unrighteousness, but Rejoices with the Truth

Love avoids sin and partners with truth. In every situation in life, love seeks that which is right and doesn't resort to sinful solutions or responses. As you seek to put your life on a new track and bring it into balance, you will be tempted to bend the rules and compromise the truth. You might be tempted to make choices or take shortcuts that take you outside the boundaries of God's Word. Love chooses to say no to such shortcuts. Love lives according to Scripture, period.

Love Bears All Things, Believes All Things, Hopes All Things, Endures All Things

These words from 1 Corinthians 13:7 are quoted a lot at weddings, but they apply to far more than just marriages—they apply to all of life. *Love hangs tough and perseveres.* For love to believe all things means that love has real *convictions* and communicates *confidence* to others. Love is optimistic and smiles at the future. And for love to endure all things means it will always remain *loyal,* even if it hurts to do so.

Love Never Fails

Whatever you do in life, if you love as a gift, you're taking the right approach. You're going to be successful—maybe not in the eyes of the world, but definitely in the eyes of God. He is always pleased when our thoughts, words, and actions are accompanied by authentic, godly, and sacrificial love. In everything you do, check your heart and ask yourself, "Am I doing this out of love? Am I bartering, or am I looking to bless others?" Try loving others as defined in 1 Corinthians 13, and you won't be disappointed with the outcome!

The Practice of Love

So how do we put our love into action? How can we make God's kind of love more than words on a page and make it real in our lives? Here are three practical principles to get you started:

Love is of God, not man, so get connected.

As the Bible says, "God is love" (1 John 4:16), and without His help, we are not able to love others as we should. It's only by the Holy Spirit's power in our lives that we can manifest God's kind of love. He indwells you as a follower of Christ, and you need Him.

First John chapter 4 lays it out clearly:

> *Beloved, let us love one another, for love is*
> *from God; and everyone who loves is born of*
> *God and knows God. The one who does not*
> *love does not know God, for God is love.…*
> *Beloved, if God so loved us, we also ought to*
> *love one another. No one has seen God at any*
> *time; if we love one another, God abides in*
> *us, and His love is perfected in us. By this we*
> *know that we abide in Him and He in us,*
> *because He has given us of His Spirit*
> *(verses 7-8,11-13).*

It's very clear that true, authentic love is rooted in the person of God Himself, and it's resourced by His power. Apart from Him, we can't exhibit it in our life. He is our role model, and Jesus on the cross is the ultimate picture of this kind of love. And if we're not showing such love to others, or even growing in our capacity to love, then there's a chance we aren't really "born of God" (verse 7). If the God of love abides in us, we should be seeing growth as we learn to love as a gift. It is one tangible demonstration of His divine presence in our life.

If you placed your faith in Christ as your Savior, then God, who is love, wants to remold you into a more loving person. As human beings, all believers still struggle with sin, and we all are indeed unloving at times. Yet the new predominant pattern of our life should be one of love toward others. Not just better bartering with love, but more giving away love as a gift. This means loving the unlovely and those who never love in return.

This new capacity for love comes from God alone. If we're not walking with Him, we're not going to be able to show this kind of love. The fruit of His Spirit, who indwells you, is love. But remember, it is His fruit, not yours. You can't just whip yourself into shape and into loving others. Jesus put it this way: "He who abides in Me and I in him, he bears much fruit, for apart from Me you can do nothing" (John 15:5). So before you go any further in your efforts to take back your life, if you aren't a Christian, then stop and commit yourself to Christ. Receive Him as your Savior. Trust Him as your Lord. Let His Spirit become your guide every step of the way. It is the only way. Pray with me:

> *Lord Jesus, thank You for dying for my sins on the cross. I place my trust in You today and ask You to be my personal Savior and Lord. I need You and trust in You today. Teach me how to love and live as You desire, and according to Your great plan for my life. Dear Lord, strengthen me, by Your Spirit within me, to love as a gift the way You loved me. In Jesus' name I pray. Amen.*

If you prayed that prayer and want help growing in your new relationship with Jesus Christ, attend a good church in your city and begin the adventure of growing spiritually with others who honor Christ and His Word. For additional resources on growing as a follower of Christ, you can also contact me through Dale Burke Leadership at www.daleburke.com.

Love is an action, not a feeling, so just do it.

The apostle John encourages us with the admonishment,

"Little children, let us not love with word or with tongue, but in deed and truth" (1 John 3:18). So often we hear the sentiment that love is a feeling. As such, it is out of our control. It's either there or missing. We even speak of "falling in or out of love" or "being captured by love" or being "bitten by the love bug." Now, we must acknowledge that the emotions of love are real and powerful. But as long as your love is controlled and lead by your emotions, you will never be able to love in the way God intends. Love must become a *choice* you make—even if you don't feel like it. Feelings are great, and God created them and possesses them Himself. But always remember this:

Feelings make great followers
but lousy leaders.

If you show love to others only when you feel like it, you are actually bartering your love—loving others as a wage or a bribe. God commands us to love as a gift, as an act of grace. He is the source of such unconditional love, and we experience it daily as we taste His grace and forgiveness. With the help of His Spirit, we can learn to give His love to others even when they don't deserve it. That's grace-based love. But we must make a deliberate choice to "just do it," whether we feel like it or not. What's amazing about loving others unconditionally is that once we deliberately set out to just do it, the very act of doing so tends to generate within us renewed feelings of love and affection.

Now, I'm not denying the reality of the negative feelings that we all experience. At times we feel hurt, angry, disappointed, frustrated, irritated, or disrespected. And when that happens, it is human nature to not *feel* a lot of love for someone. So what should we do? The key is to remember the different expressions of love as stated in Scripture. For example, one form of love is "speaking the truth in love" (Ephesians 4:15). If you don't tell the truth and express how you feel, bitterness will take root in your heart and choke out any feelings of love.

So as you choose to show kindness, gentleness, compassion, forgiveness, or any of the other positive actions of love, don't forget that love also speaks the truth when it feels angry. Tell that associate, spouse, child, or friend, "I care about our relationship, so you need to know that when you (describe their hurtful act), I feel (describe your negative feelings)." Then forgive that person and choose to show love in spite of the way you feel!

Love is a gift, not a wage or a bribe, so give it freely.
Love is a gift. It is to be given away freely without expectation of anything in return. Don't use love as a *wage*, paying back those who first loved you. Jesus said in Luke 6:32, "If you love those who love you, what credit is that to you? For even sinners love those who love them."

Jesus then added, "If you lend to those from whom you expect to receive, what credit is that to you? Even sinners lend to sinners in order to receive back the same amount" (verse 34). Some people use love as a *bribe*—even in their marriages. They'll do something nice for someone else in the hopes of getting something nice in return. That's bribery, not love.

Jesus then went on to describe what true love does: "Love your enemies, and do good, and lend, expecting nothing in return; and your reward will be great, and you will be sons of the Most High; for He Himself is kind to ungrateful and evil men." That's supernatural love—the kind that gives generously without any care for something in return. If you want to excel at love, this is the key! If you want to take back your life, love like God and watch how life changes right before your eyes!

The Reward of Love

When we give love as a gift, look what happens, according to Scripture: "Give, and it will be given to you. They will pour into your lap a good measure—pressed down, shaken together, and running over. For by your standard of measure it will be measured to you in return" (verse 38). Wow, what a promise! When you give love away, you put yourself in the best position to be loved in return. If you want to receive more love, then start loving as a gift. Just do it! You have the ultimate example before you in Jesus Christ, who died on the cross for you, a sinner. You can choose, as you walk with Christ, to love as He loves. You can choose to love as a gift. It will revolutionize your relationships. Try it, and see how much better it makes your life!

CHOICE #3:
DON'T BARTER WITH LOVE—GIVE IT AWAY

Chapter Summary: Get the Big Idea

Jesus simplified life and redirected our priorities with the second half of His Great Commandment—love God, and love people. Then He radically redefined love as a gift, a true "give-away" instead of a tool for bartering our way to success. With the help of His Spirit and wisdom of His Word, you can reset your priorities and redefine your love. Get started today and choose love as a gift and people as your personal priority.

Questions to Guide Discussion and Your Choices

1. We all are guilty of using love as a wage or a bribe. We learn it from birth, and our prideful hearts track that way naturally. When and where do you tend to slip into such use of love in your relationships?

2. Giving love as a gift, with no strings attached, is how God loved us on the cross. Think of one or two examples of how such love can enhance and freshen your closest relationships. (If married, with your spouse...if single, your closest friendships.)

3. The chapter surveys God's definition of love as described in 1 Corinthians 13. In which of these attitudes or actions are you strong? In which areas do you need to focus for greater growth?

4. People are to be our priority. What obstacles do you need to overcome to make sure your family and friends are a priority over work or business?

5. List at least one change in your schedule that you intend to make right away to protect quality fun time with your family and closest friends.

6. Is there a broken relationship that needs to be healed with forgiveness and gace? If so, take the first step, call or write, and give grace to someone today.

TAKE BACK YOUR LIFE!

Choice #1: Stop Climbing
Start Down the Ladder to Success

Choice #2: Let God Be God
Build the Ultimate Alliance

Choice #3: Don't Barter with Love—Give It Away
Make Love Your Gift and People Your Priority

Choice #4: Serve Your Way to Success
Nurture a Servant Spirit

Choice #5: Chase a Better Dream
Capture God's Vision for Life

Choice #6: Build a Life-Team
Never Tackle Life Alone

Choice #7: Play to Your Strengths
Stop Trying to Do It All

Choice #8: Improve Your Flex-ability
Be a Lifelong Learner

Choice #9: Slow Down and Focus
Do One Thing at a Time

Choice #10: Nurture Sanctified Stubbornness
Keep the Faith No Matter What

WARNING:
Pride says, "What's in it for me?"

TAKE-BACK TIP #4:
Humility says, "What can I do for you?"

SERVE YOUR WAY TO SUCCESS

Nurture a

Servant Spirit

Three of the most common words in the English language happen to be among the shortest. They are *me*, *my*, and *mine*. Do you remember how early in life you learned those words? Anyone who has children knows these words rank right near the top, near *da-da* and *ma-ma*. Early in life, right from the womb, our sin nature whispers into our ears, "You are the center of the universe." And before long, we begin to believe that life is all about us. It's one of the reasons My Life grows and goes out of control.

The Monster loves the sound of these "m" words. Why? Because if life is "all about me," then our pride drives us to climb for success. It empowers the Monster and keeps our lives out of control. If you want to take back your life, get it back under control and nurture humility. Humility weakens the Monster and empowers real success. It calls us to let God be God and surrender control to Him. And it calls us to think and act like a servant. Without nurturing humility, you will never take back your life.

The Essence of Pride

Recently I came across a list called "Toddler's Rules of Possession." See if you can't relate to these:

1. If I like it, it's mine.

2. If it's in my hand, it's mine.

3. If I can take it from you, it's mine.

4. If I had it a little while ago, it's mine.

5. If it's mine, it must NEVER appear to be yours in any way.

6. If I'm doing or building something, all the pieces are mine.

7. If it looks just like mine, it's mine.

8. If I saw it first, it's mine.

9. If you are playing with something and you put it down, it automatically becomes mine.

10. If it's broken, it's yours.[4]

We may laugh at these, but there is more truth in that list than we want to admit! While these rules truthfully and humorously depict our children at play, they also truthfully but not so humorously depict our own behavior in our homes, offices, churches, and neighborhoods. Once again, at the root of this all-too-common selfishness is our number-one enemy: pride. It keeps raising its ugly head as we move to recapture life as God designed it.

And Jesus, with even more certainty, taught, "If you want to be great, be a servant." Being a servant, as Jesus was, requires real humility.

The Essence of Humility

So what *is* humility? What does it mean to not be proud?

Is humility the opposite of pride? While humility may morally oppose pride in that it is a virtue while pride is a vice, humility is not by definition the opposite of pride. Pride is defined as thinking too highly of oneself, and if humility were the opposite of pride, then humility would be defined as having a low opinion of oneself. Yet Jesus Christ, as the Son of God, was the perfect model of humility, and He didn't hold to a low view of Himself. So what exactly is humility? Here's what one Bible dictionary says:

> **HUMILITY CAN HELP FLUSH THE VENOM OF PRIDE OUT OF OUR VEINS.**

> HUMILITY (Heb. 'anawa, "gentleness, affliction," also from 'ana, "to be bowed down"; Grk. tapeinophrosune, "lowliness of mind," praotes, "gentleness"). Humility in the spiritual sense is an inwrought grace of the soul that allows one to think of himself no more highly than he ought to think (Eph 4:1-2; Col 3:12-13; cf. Rom 12:3).[5]

I would propose that at the heart of humility is a willingness to "bow low" and serve others. It does not need to be first, to be adored, to be lifted up as the center of attention, *even if it deserves all of the above.* Christ certainly deserved adoration, attention, and admiration. Yet in humility He chose the role and demeanor of a servant. He didn't give up His strengths. He never quit being the Son of God. He used His strengths for others. Humility serves with its best stuff while acknowledging that all our best stuff comes as gifts from God.

A Correct View of Humility

To be humble does not mean viewing oneself as worthless or having little to offer. Rather, a humble believer needs to have a true and informed perspective, an objective evaluation, of both his or her strengths and weaknesses. Before servants can be of maximum value to those who are being served, they need to be fully aware of the gifts and abilities God has entrusted to them. If in false humility they feel they have little to offer, they will be of little value to anyone.

Humility has a buffering effect on pride. As we become humbler, we become less prideful, and vice versa. Therefore, humility can help flush the venom of pride out of our veins.

Humility's antidotal effects on pride may be misunderstood as producing weakness, leaving us vulnerable to abuse or defeat. Some of us may fear that nurturing humility will lead to failure in the various endeavors of life. Others fear it is the first step toward mediocre performance, career stagnation, and abusive treatment in our relationships. In other words, does humility turn us into gutless wimps? Absolutely not! Again, Christ is our model for true humility, and He was certainly no wimp! Don't fear humility; pursue it!

Humility a Mark of Greatness

The world's mind-set typically perceives that the most successful leaders are ruthlessly ambitious egomaniacs who shove aside all who get between them and the top rung of the ladder to success. But recent evidence gives a different testimony. The leaders in many of the best businesses and organizations today possess a spirit of humility. In his landmark book *Good to Great,* Jim Collins reports the surprise he felt when the research on top executives of "good to great" companies came in:

> We were surprised, shocked really, to discover the type of leadership required for turning a good company into a great one. Compared to high-profile leaders with big personalities who make headlines and become celebrities, the good-to-great leaders seem to have come from Mars. Self-effacing, quiet, reserved, even shy—these leaders are a paradoxical blend of personal *humility* (emphasis added) and professional will.[6]

Do you see yourself struggling with too much pride and not enough humility? Do you expect others to wait on you or do you look for a chance to serve others? Are you more of a master or a servant? If we're honest, we will all admit that at times we struggle with pride. And if we want to take the "humility" step down the ladder of success, we first need to admit that pride is an ever-present enemy in our life. We need to weed out pride and work at cultivating a servant's heart.

So how can we learn to spot the weeds of pride?

The Warning Signs of Pride

We often don't recognize it, but pride creeps into every aspect of our lives, including our relationships with other people. Pride manifests itself in various ways. One of the most common is when we catch ourselves thinking, *What's in it for me?* We seldom say it, but we think it; and we make our choices based on the answer.

Pride says, "What's in it for me?*"*

Here are four more warning signs that pride is alive and well in our life:

It's all about me—Pride keeps us walled up in our own world, where we are the only one who matters. However, humility says, "This is God's world, and I'm sharing it with others who have needs, too."

Look out for number one—Pride not only tells you that it is all about you, but it reminds you that you and your needs reign supreme. Pride says, "Watch your backside as you climb, and don't let anyone pass you up." Humility says, "Look back and see if anyone is being left behind. Reach back and give them a hand."

I deserve a break today—Pride says, "I deserve a break. I deserve better. I deserve more pay, a better life, more toys." This attitude comes from a spirit of want, which turns blessings into rights.

Humility sees the good life as an unwarranted blessing, a gracious gift from God, and a prompt for praise instead of pride.

I can do it alone—Pride says, "I don't need anyone's help." Pride leaves no room for God as the Ultimate Giver of all good gifts. It creates the illusion of self-sufficiency. Humility recognizes the hand of God, seen or unseen, in all good gifts.

The Divine Warnings About Pride

Scripture warns us repeatedly to watch out for this deadly disease of the soul. God obviously knows how easily pride can go undetected in our lives. So He warns us of pride and its dangers. Before we casually brush off His warnings, we need to humbly look into our hearts and face the cold, hard facts:

Pride is Enemy #1 and even on our best days,
it lurks just under the surface of our souls, looking for
any opportunity to reassert itself and take control.

One of the more well-known verses on pride is Proverbs 16:18: "Pride goes before destruction, and a haughty spirit before stumbling." And 1 Corinthians 10:12 warns, "Let him who thinks he stands take heed that he does not fall." So if you are sure pride is not *your* problem, guess what? You just confirmed its presence! Go back and read the last few pages.

Humility says, "What can I do for you?"

Pride says, "What can you do for me?" But humility seeks to serve others. What does it mean to be a servant? For most in our culture, the concept of servanthood provokes unpleasant images of slavery or indentured servitude. Before we define what it means to be a servant, let's first confront some of the common misperceptions about serving others.

Correcting Misconceptions About Servanthood

Philippians chapter 2 is a great place to start if you want to blow away the foggy thinking about servanthood. Philippians 2:3-11 says,

> *Do nothing from selfishness or empty conceit, but with humility of mind regard one another as more important than yourselves; do not merely look out for your own personal interests, but also for the interests of others. Have this attitude in yourselves which was also in Christ Jesus, who, although He existed in the form of God, did not regard equality with God a thing to be grasped, but emptied Himself, taking the form of a bond-servant, and being made in the likeness of men. Being found in appearance as a man, He humbled Himself by becoming obedient to the point of death, even death on a cross. For this reason also, God highly exalted Him, and bestowed on Him the name which is above every name, so that at the name of Jesus every knee will bow, of those who are in heaven and on earth and under the earth, and that every tongue will confess that Jesus Christ is Lord, to the glory of God the Father.*

Wow! That is one potent bit of wisdom on servanthood. Let's use it to compare and contrast our world's concept of serving others in a spirit of true servanthood as modeled by Jesus. Here it is in a nutshell:

Worldly Service	True Servanthood
Attitudes	
Heart of pride	Heart of humility
Focus on me	Focus on others
Need to impress	Nothing to prove
Lives to get	Lives to give
Self-exaltation	God's exaltation

Serving Others

For the weak or unskilled	For the strong and gifted
Taken from me	Given by me
Produces frustration	Produces fulfillment
Resentful doormat	Joyful sacrifice

First, the attitudes of the prideful servant are radically different from those of the humble one. He may serve, but only if it's in his best interest. His operative question is always, What's in it for me? Impressing others and making himself look good motivates his actions. He tries to avoid serving unless it helps him get ahead. He believes servanthood is the plight of the weak and leads to frustration. He is afraid that people will treat him as a doormat if he takes the role of the servant. He avoids it at all costs unless it helps him climb the ladder.

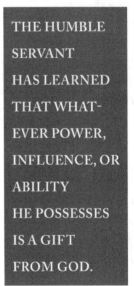

THE HUMBLE SERVANT HAS LEARNED THAT WHATEVER POWER, INFLUENCE, OR ABILITY HE POSSESSES IS A GIFT FROM GOD.

The humble servant, like Christ, does not fear serving those above or below him. He serves as a lifestyle at work, at home, in the community, anywhere, and anytime. Why? Because his heart has nurtured humility. He has learned that whatever power, influence, or ability he possesses is a gift from God. He is secure in God's love and acceptance of him, so he has nothing to prove and no one to impress. He finds joy in giving his best away in service. His goal is to glorify God, and he knows God will exalt him in due time if He so desires. So this servant gives himself away and senses joy and fulfillment in doing so. He views service as an opportunity to use his God-given strengths for others.

When Jesus died on the cross, He wasn't out to get anything for Himself. He humbled Himself and died willingly because He wanted to give glory to His Father and salvation to us on earth. While it's true that the Father exalted Jesus after the crucifixion and resurrection, that exaltation wasn't Jesus' motive for going to the cross.

What makes Jesus such a great example is that He is the second person of the Godhead—He is God the Son. That means He deserves all our worship and service. Yet He emptied Himself, took on the form of a bondservant, gave of Himself to others, and died on the cross. And in the end, God highly exalted Him. That's the wonderful paradox about serving others in humility:

> *When you serve in* humility,
> *you end up being* exalted.
> *And when you serve in order to* exalt *yourself,*
> *you end up being* humbled.

Pulling It All Together

Romans 12:3 provides a balanced perspective on pride, humility, and how we are to think about ourselves. To set the context, the apostle Paul has just reminded us in verses 1-2 that the first step down the ladder to success is to surrender—to let God be God and offer ourselves to Him in service. Paul wrote, "I urge you brethren, by the mercies of God, to present your bodies a living and holy sacrifice, acceptable to God, which is your spiritual service of worship. And do not be conformed to this world, but be transformed by the renewing of your mind."

Then right on the heels of this truth comes Romans 12:3, which challenges us to move away from pride and serve others in humility:

> *I say to everyone among you not to think more*
> *highly of himself than he ought to think [less*
> *pride]; but to think so as to have sound*
> *judgment [know the truth about yourself],*
> *as God has allotted to each a measure of faith*
> *[it's a gift, so be humble].*

Here we see pride defined as thinking more highly of yourself than you ought. Then comes the corrective response: Think with sound judgment about yourself. And what truth do we need to remember? We all have different measures of faith as gifts from God. So don't take pride in your gifts, but also don't deny their existence! Thank God for the gifts and abilities and opportunities He has given to you, and get to work using them to serve one another. Verse 4-8 then go on to describe the various gifts that empower our service to others. Here's the point:

Humility is never the denial of ability, but
the recognition that our abilities are gifts from
God that empower our service toward others.

In other words, humility gives credit where credit is due—to the Giver of the gifts. God wants you to be fully aware of your strengths, but you must also acknowledge that these strengths came from God. You might say humility is proud, but it is proud of the Giver instead of the gifts.

Now that we know what servanthood is not, we're ready for the next question: What would life look like, if we began to serve others in the same way Jesus did? Let's look at His example, and see what we can learn.

Servanthood: Life as It Was Meant to Be

Created to Worship and Serve God

From the very beginning of time, God intended for all of us to serve. Even if humankind had not fallen into sin, still, God's original design was for us to show humility and possess a servant spirit. God informs us of this in Scripture:

Shout joyfully to the LORD, all the earth. Serve
the LORD with gladness; come before Him
with joyful singing. Know that the LORD

Himself is God; it is He who has made us, and
not we ourselves; we are His people and the
sheep of His pasture (Psalm 100:1-3).

Pride tells us we are self-made, but the psalmist reminds us there is no such thing as a self-made man or woman. God made us, and He continues to shape us throughout our life. He makes our achievements possible. Thus none of us can take the credit for "making it" in life. True humility acknowledges we are who we are because of the goodness and grace of God.

> SERVICE IS ONE OF THE ULTIMATE ACTS OF LOVE.

Created to Work and Serve Others
In Colossians 3:22-24, Paul wrote,

> *Slaves, in all things obey those who are your*
> *masters on earth, not with external service,*
> *as those who merely please men, but with sin-*
> *cerity of heart, fearing the Lord. Whatever*
> *you do, do your work heartily, as for the Lord*
> *rather than for men, knowing that from the*
> *Lord you will receive the reward of the inheri-*
> *tance. It is the Lord Christ whom you serve.*

Note that the apostle Paul speaks not only to everyday citizens, but also to slaves. Paul was not endorsing slavery here; rather, he was saying, "Even if you're a slave, and even if you have a bad boss or a tough job, remember that it's really the Lord Jesus Christ whom you serve." No matter whether your boss is fair or unfair, appreciative or arrogant, we are created and called to serve as if serving Jesus Himself.

So the next time you get a crummy assignment at work—one that you think is beneath you—how should you respond? See the task as a way to serve Christ and tackle it with a servant spirit. You might not want to do that assignment for a human boss, but doing it for your divine Savior, your Ultimate Boss, puts the task in a different light. And as you bring this kind of joyful serving spirit into the workplace, you glorify Christ and you grow as a Christian. In fact, one of the best places we as Christians can learn to grow spiritually is on the job because of all the challenges we face. Those challenges become much more manageable and meaningful when we do them with the attitude that we're serving Christ.

And what if you *are* the boss? Colossians 3:22-24 applies to everyone up and down the corporate ladder. Bosses should also live to serve and focus on meeting the needs of others.

Created to Relate and Love by Serving

Here's another passage from Paul that describes the nature of servanthood:

> *You were called to freedom, brethren; only do*
> *not turn your freedom into an opportunity for*
> *the flesh, but through love serve one another.*
> *For the whole Law is fulfilled in one word, in*
> *the statement, "You shall love your neighbor as*
> *yourself" (Galatians 5:13-14).*

Here Paul equates *serving* your neighbor with *loving* your neighbor. After all, service is one of the ultimate acts of love because it requires self-sacrifice—sacrifice of time, of energy, and of priority. When you sacrifice for the ones you love, you freshen the relationship. And again, the upside of such servanthood is that it tends to return the favor (of course, that shouldn't be our motive for serving). Love as a gift and not a wage or a bribe, and love will come back! Try it at work, at home, everywhere.

Created to Imitate God and Jesus Christ, the Ultimate Servant

Jesus Himself made it abundantly clear that true success comes from going down the ladder:

*Whoever wishes to become great among you
shall be your servant, and whoever wishes to
be first among you shall be your slave
(Matthew 20:26-27).*

Just as Jesus paradoxically found His glory in becoming a servant, so can we. Servanthood may be lowly by the world's standards, but in the heavenly paradigm, servanthood rivals nobility. The serving life, then, is the good life. It is the life God intended for us. And all this time, the world has been telling us the opposite. We've been told that the good life comes to those who look out for themselves. That's a lie. God created us to serve, and through service we discover real joy and fulfillment.

Ways to Nurture Humility

What is the key to cultivating a humble spirit? Below are seven suggestions. As you work your way through them, you will find yourself shifting gears and becoming more humble in your approach to everything you do. With these suggestions you can decide how to better serve your spouse, your kids, your employer, your church, your neighbor, and others. You'll also want to ask God to bring to your mind specific ideas about how you can serve those around you. And as you put these suggestions into practice, you're going to see some amazing changes take place in your life.

Here they are:

1. Study God, the omni-everything

2. Study the fruit of the Spirit

3. Focus on grace

4. Examine yourself and search your heart in prayer

5. Listen to honest feedback about your strengths and weaknesses

6. Embrace suffering and learn from it

7. Just go ahead and serve!

Take a lesson from Jesus. The most powerful, revered, and respected man who ever walked the face of the earth. He served with humility. Are you willing to put others before yourself and serve them? If so, then you are ready to take the next step toward life as it was meant to be!

CHOICE #4: **SERVE YOUR WAY TO SUCCESS**

Chapter Summary: Get the Big Idea

Jesus shocked His followers and redefined the road to success when He declared, "If you want to be great, be a servant." Pride tells us to look out for #1. Humility calls us to look out for the other person. We're to look for ways to meet other people's needs. This radical approach to life—thinking and acting as a servant—not only makes you nicer, it also makes you greater! Choose it today.

Questions to Guide Discussion and Your Choices

1. What did you learn in the chapter about the profile and manifestations of pride? Where and when does pride most often surface in our life? In your life?

2. What is the essence of humility, and how does it manifest itself in our life? What has God used in your life to humble you?

3. Reflect on the misconceptions about servanthood in today's culture. How is it most misunderstood, and where have you observed this lack of understanding?

4. What did you learn from the study of Romans 12 and the essence of real humility? Why is it important for the humble servant to have an accurate view of himself—both his strengths and weaknesses?

5. Review the list that illustrates the benefits of humility over pride. How does this prove that the humble person, in every area of life, actually has a competitive edge over others?

6. How can we nurture humility in our character and our conduct? Look at the list on pages 85-86. What will you focus on to help grow your personal humility factor.

TAKE BACK YOUR LIFE!

Choice #1:   Stop Climbing
Start Down the Ladder to Success

Choice #2:   Let God Be God
Build the Ultimate Alliance

Choice #3:   Don't Barter with Love—Give It Away
Make Love Your Gift and People Your Priority

Choice #4:   Serve Your Way to Success
Nurture a Servant Spirit

Choice #5:   Chase a Better Dream
Capture God's Vision for Life

Choice #6:   Build a Life-Team
Never Tackle Life Alone

Choice #7:   Play to Your Strengths
Stop Trying to Do It All

Choice #8:   Improve Your Flex-ability
Be a Lifelong Learner

Choice #9:   Slow Down and Focus
Do One Thing at a Time

Choice #10:   Nurture Sanctified Stubbornness
Keep the Faith No Matter What

WARNING:
Pride says, "Why bother?
It's good enough."

TAKE-BACK TIP #5:
Humility says, "Lord, what
are Your *dreams for me?"*

CHASE A BETTER DREAM

Capture God's

Vision for Life

Martin Luther King Jr.'s famous words "I have a dream" continually reverberate in the schools, minds, and history books of our country, leaving a lasting reminder of the importance of dreams and the value of chasing big ones. Listen to just a few of his famous words as if you were hearing them on August 28, 1963, with the Lincoln Memorial in the background:

> I have a dream that one day this nation will rise up and live out the true meaning of its creed: "We hold these truths to be self-evident: that all men are created equal."

> I have a dream that one day on the red hills of Georgia the sons of former slaves and the sons of former slave owners will be able to sit down together at the table of brotherhood.[7]

He went on to describe in vivid word pictures a new America, one radically different from the world of the 1950s and 1960s when blacks and whites could not live, or eat, or study together. With nine "I have a dream..." statements, he painted a vivid picture of a new life in a new land. And then he concluded the speech with a confident declaration of hope:

> And when this happens, when we allow freedom to ring,
> when we let it ring from every village and every hamlet,
> from every state and every city,
> we will be able to speed up that day when all of God's children,
> black men and white men, Jews and Gentiles,
> Protestants and Catholics, will be able to join hands
> and sing in the words of the old Negro spiritual,
> "Free at last! Free at last! Thank God Almighty,
> we are free at last!" [8]

People were mobilized by King's dream. And one year later the Civil Rights Act of 1964 was passed.

SMALL PEOPLE WITH BIG DREAMS CAN MAKE A DIFFERENCE, IF THE DREAM IS THE RIGHT ONE.

History is full of great people who began life as ordinary individuals with extraordinary dreams. Small people with big dreams can make a difference, if the dream is the right one. But they became great not only by dreaming, but by getting out of bed day after day to relentlessly pursue their vision of change. They chased their dreams until they crossed the threshold from fantasy into reality. The lives of many of our heroes, such as the founding fathers of America, Thomas Edison, the Wright brothers, and Amelia Earhart demonstrate the truth that great lives begin with good dreams. They all, like Martin Luther King Jr., had a dream and chased it.

On a personal level, everyone needs a dream. You need a picture of what could be, of what does not exist today. You need an image of a "new you" with a "new life," experiencing life as it was meant to be lived when God created our relatives, Adam and Eve, and blessed them in the garden—a dream of you remade into the image of Jesus Christ. You must not define your future by your past.

As Christians, we certainly have a reason to dream, to envision what could be true of our lives. After all, we have a Lord who promises and predicts amazing things for those who call Him Father. The Christian life should be a constant pursuit of new dreams and goals. Since the ultimate goal is to be like Jesus and emulate His life, we will never fully arrive until we are perfected in His presence in heaven. So whenever a dream is realized, a horizon reached, the journey continues. There is always another new dream, another new horizon, if you are traveling and dreaming with Christ. Just as a boat sailing across water continuously approaches new and changing horizons, so also do we as believers find ever-new spiritual horizons and higher goals for every aspect of our lives.

Dreams vs. Memories

My former professor, mentor, and friend Dr. Howard Hendricks warns, "When your memories are more exciting than your dreams, you've begun to die." I find this statement convicting because I'm often tempted to only dream to the level of my best memories. I find myself happy to simply maintain and hold my ground and not be overwhelmed by My Life. But according to Hendricks, that's not dreaming, that's dying! God wants my dreams to always be more exciting than my memories. That's faith. That's hope. That's the power of dreaming with God.

What about you? Do you have dreams you're pursuing as you journey with God? Or are you content to relive the best of your memories? If you want to take back your life, you must dream new dreams. You must dream God's dreams. If you don't, you may find yourself chasing a nightmare instead of a dream! The world entices us with dreams that don't deliver what they promise. Chasing the wrong dreams can turn your life into a nightmare. So make sure you prayerfully and carefully define the dream before you pursue it.

Dreaming: Empty Hype or Real Hope?

What makes a good dream? Is it really worth the effort, or are we just fooling ourselves to make ourselves feel better about life? Sure, leaders like Martin Luther King Jr. have a great dream, but I'm just an average Joe trying to make it to the next day! But it is our dreams about the future that carry us through today. They energize us and stimulate our growth.

A dream is a vision or picture of you or your life not as it is, not as it has been, but as it was meant to be.

A firm and confident faith that tomorrow can and will be different from today can empower and direct us as we tackle life. Hebrews 11:1-2,6 calls us to chase God's dreams if we hope to please our heavenly Father:

*Faith is the assurance of things hoped for,
the conviction of things not seen.
For by it the men of old gained approval....
And without faith it is impossible to please Him.*

I'm not suggesting false *hype,* but real *hope.* I'm not advocating a "power of positive thinking" that denies the negatives of life. I'm not suggesting you live in a *fantasy world,* but that you redefine the *real world* to include the presence and power of a real and really great God! If you're a child of God, it makes sense to possess a faith-based and God-sized dream of real change and growth in your life. Take heart in knowing that according to Hebrews 11:1-2,6, we can have "assurance" and "conviction" that real change and growth can and will take place. So if you struggle with Life and the Monster has you on the run or on the defensive, here is a promise: With Christ, you can take back your life. Change is coming!

However, we live in a fallen world in which our old self often derails our attempts to live life as it was meant to be. So why should we even attempt to dream with confidence that our future can truly be different? For most of us, past dreams and prayers could fill a book, or a whole series of books, with frustrated memories. We feel like we are doomed to failure before we even start. Who needs one more disappointment? But that is not God talking; rather, it's your Old Life, the Monster created by your past pursuit of the world's dreams. It loves to pull out your Book of Past Failures and read to you at night. So when you are reminded of the frustrating chapters of your past, stop listening and pick up God's Book of Dreams and read Ephesians 3:20-21:

> WE ARE ABLE TO DREAM BIG, AND MORE IMPORTANTLY, ACCOMPLISH BIG DREAMS, BECAUSE WE HAVE A BIG GOD.

Now to Him who is able to do far more abundantly beyond all that we ask or think, according to the power that works within us, to Him be the glory in the church and in Christ Jesus to all generations forever and ever. Amen.

We are able to dream big, and more importantly, accomplish big dreams because we have a big God who is able to do "far more abundantly beyond all that we ask or think." That means no dream of "life as it's meant to be" surpasses God's ability. There is always a new dream of what the Lord can do in our future. And along the lines of what Howard Hendricks said, why rest on memories of the past when we have the power and confidence through Christ to dream bigger for the future?

The promise in Ephesians 3:20-21 calls every follower of

Christ to dream new dreams. Whether you are a new Christian or you have been walking with God for 80 years, whether you're in a tough stretch or at the mountaintop, God is ready to work in and through each of us. He only asks that we be willing to let Him. We can and should have a vision for what God has yet to do both *in* us and *through* us.

One of the most empowering disciplines for breaking free of My Life as it exists today is to dream with God and believe that by His strength, it can change. I can't always promise that every dream you dream with God will come true. Life is more complex than that, and besides, I'm not God! But I can promise you that if you fail to even dream it, it will not come true. So let's start dreaming new dreams of life under control, lived as it was meant to be!

To Dream with God—Remember the Basics

Christ Died Not Only to Redeem Us, but to Remake Us

Man and woman were made in the image of God. When they fell into sin, that image became corrupted. We need not only forgiveness, but freedom to be remade into the men and women we were meant to be. And great news! Christ not only redeemed us from the *penalty of sin*, but from the *power of sin* as well. His dream for His children is to remake them, every single one, into new creatures, new creations of grace, shaped into His image. Now that's a great dream! Reflect on these verses and note what happens to us as a result of becoming a Christian:

> *2 Corinthians 5:17*—"If anyone is in Christ, he is a new creature; the old things passed away; behold, new things have come."
>
> *2 Peter 1:2-4*—"Grace and peace be multiplied to you in the knowledge of God and of Jesus our Lord; seeing that His divine power has granted to us everything

pertaining to life and godliness, through the true knowledge of Him who called us by His own glory and excellence. For by these He has granted to us precious and magnificent promises, so that by them you may become partakers of the divine nature."

> HE IS ABLE TO DO FAR MORE THAN WE CAN IMAGINE, SO LET'S START IMAGINING MORE!

Galatians 5:16—"Walk by the Spirit, and you will not carry out the desire of the flesh."

Galatians 5:22-23—"The fruit of the Spirit is love, joy, peace, patience, kindness, goodness, faithfulness, gentleness, self-control." As you abide in Christ, the Spirit produces good fruit in your life. This fruit attests to the work He is doing in you.

Ephesians 3:20-21—"Now to Him who is able to do far more abundantly beyond all that we ask or think, according to the power that works within us, to Him be the glory in the church and in Christ Jesus to all generations forever and ever. Amen."

This is reality—you can count on it! God has no desire to wait until heaven to fix you and your life. He wants the transformation to start now. Granted, part of His grand restoration plan will be fulfilled only when He remakes heaven and earth in eternity. But our personal restoration begins now, not in heaven. And He is able to do far more than we can imagine, so let's start imagining more!

We've All Got a Long Way to Go

God's work in us isn't quick and easy. We live on a fallen planet, in fallen bodies, surrounded by fallen people, with sinful remnants of our old life still struggling to take us back to life as it's always been! On top of everything else we have a spiritual enemy who tempts us to chase the lesser dreams of this world. So understand that our restoration in Christ is a lifelong process.

At times we all face failure. At times we all regress. At times we all feel disappointed in others and ourselves, and even in God. That's why God invented G-R-A-C-E. Learn grace, love grace, embrace grace. Give it generously to yourself and others. You will need it more than ever as you set new goals, dream fresh dreams, and pursue them with renewed passion. Grace will free you from past failures and keep you in the game when you're tempted to quit. You will need it when you realize, "Oh heavenly Father…I failed again."

As we abide more in Christ, feed upon God's Word, and persevere through experiences that shape and polish us, we grow spiritually. The apostle Paul spoke about this process in Philippians 3:12-14:

> *Not that I have already obtained it or have*
> *already become perfect, but I press on so that*
> *I may lay hold of that for which also I was*
> *laid hold of by Christ Jesus. Brethren, I do not*
> *regard myself as having laid hold of it yet; but*
> *one thing I do: forgetting what lies behind and*
> *reaching forward to what lies ahead, I press on.*

Paul, of all people in the Bible, had one of the most spectacular life-transformations. One day as he was walking toward Damascus with the intention of killing Christians, and after seeing a light and hearing God's voice he, the killer of Christians, joined the very movement he was seeking to exterminate. However, while a lot changed in his heart and soul on his day of conversion, his transformation was a lifelong journey. Even late in life, as the greatest leader in the early church, he still viewed himself as a work in progress. How did he approach setting new dreams for his life?

Paul delared, "I press on." This verb, in the present indicative, indicates that his growth in Christ was a continuing action in real time—not just part of his past, and not just for his future. As a person of great spiritual maturity, he still had an enthusiastic vision for the future. He was "forgetting what lies behind and reaching forward to what lies ahead." That's the kind of dream we all need every day of our lives. Paul's dreams were still more exciting than his memories.

We Don't Have to Make the Journey Alone

When I said that Christ saved you not only to redeem you but to remake you, I really did mean that He, God Himself, reshapes you and your life. He does not leave us all alone to take back and remake our lives. Don't get me wrong; we are involved in the process. We have choices to make and things to do. It does take some discipline and work on our part, but it is always by God's strength that we tackle life. Don't attempt it on your own or you really will know failure! Christ yearns to work through you by His indwelling Spirit, to fulfill His dreams in you. Therefore, we can rest in the fact that it can and will be done if we allow Him to work in us. Consider John 15:4-5:

> *Abide in Me, and I in you. As the branch cannot bear fruit of itself unless it abides in the vine, so neither can you unless you abide in Me. I am the vine, you are the branches; he who abides in Me and I in him, he bears much fruit, for apart from Me you can do nothing.*

This verse contains both good news and bad news, but in the end, it gives us great news. The bad news is that apart from Christ, *you can do nothing.* We are all powerless on our own. The good news is that when you abide in Him, *you'll bear much fruit.* In the end, it is all great news because even though we have a long way to go, Christ does not leave us to succeed on our own. Christ provides every resource we need for our transformation to take place. Later in this book we will explore some of the surprising ways Christ helps us. But for now, just know He will be there for

DREAMING IS NOT ABOUT HOLDING GROUND, IT'S ABOUT MOVING FORWARD.

you, even if you can't see His hand at work. Trust me, He keeps His promises!

Progress, Not Perfection, Is Guaranteed

God's manual for dreaming, the Bible, predicts and guarantees *progress,* not *perfection.* As we saw just a moment ago in John 15:4-5, Jesus promises that He will bear much fruit in us, but only as we abide in Him. If we abide in Christ, let His Word abide in us, and live in His love and His power, we will bear fruit. He will transform us. Christ did not pledge perfection, but He does guarantee progress, and the growth of spiritual fruit in our lives bears witness to that progress. So be patient and, as I mentioned earlier, give yourself grace. Abide in His love. You'll need it as you journey toward life as it's meant to be.

Distractions That Hinder Our Dreams

Why do we as Christians often find ourselves lacking dreams for our lives? With Christ to model perfection for us, it should be easy to dream up ways in which we want to change and grow. Nevertheless, I've met a good number of Christians who have no dreams for themselves, and I admit I've found myself in that situation, too. Many of us seem to be so concerned about avoiding regression that we are perfectly content to merely hold our ground. But dreaming is not about holding ground, it's about moving forward.

Dream stoppers

• Distraction	• Frustration
• Fear	• Resignation

So what causes us to not dream? There are many hindrances we allow to get in the way, to keep us from dreaming, and here we're going to look at four of the more common ones. As you go through the following list, examine yourself. Perhaps you will identify some problems that have kept you from daring to imagine what God can do in your life.

Distraction: "I'm too busy with my other pursuits."

Chasing the dreams of this world, which actually turn life into a nightmare, keep us so busy we fail to pursue godly goals. We are chasing degrees, money, health, good looks, the next promotion, or other pleasures of planet Earth. These aren't always bad in and of themselves. But they are deadly when they distract us from the purposeful, prayerful pursuit of God's dreams for our lives, spiritual growth, and vital relationships with family and friends. These secondary priorities preoccupy us and rob us of life as it's meant to be. Before long, they assume first priority and our spiritual life takes a back seat and stagnates as we await heaven. The Monster loves it when we give up the struggle and acquiesce to Its call to climb higher in search of the pseudohappiness of our culture.

Pride: "I can change myself."

Some of us realize our need for change but instead of letting God do His work in us, we try to transform ourselves. Yet self-effort brings limited change and leaves us with a growing sense of frustration. We may clean up our outward behavior and look better to others, but we still have the same struggles with the inner person, with the heart issues that only Christ can transform. Eventually our frustration can turn into quiet despair and lead us to quit. We don't necessarily drop out of life, but we settle in and let Life set the agenda. Pride hates to admit defeat, so our pride convinces us that we're really not that bad after all—especially compared to the person across the street! This leads quite naturally to the next obstacle.

Contentment: "I'm already good enough, or even better than most."

Contentment in such areas as your financial status or life

> FAITH IS LIKE A MUSCLE. IT GROWS STRONGER ONLY WHEN IT IS STRETCHED BEYOND ITS COMFORT ZONE.

situations chases out greed and grumbling, but if you become content with your spiritual growth, you stop dreaming, and as Howard Hendricks warned, you begin to die. Those who find themselves in this condition put no effort into their spiritual lives because they have no more goals to pursue. Their motto shifts from "press on" to simply "hold on"— good is good enough. This good-enough mind-set appears most commonly among those who are veterans in the faith. They feel they've been to war, taken a few beachheads for Jesus, and even have some spiritual battle scars to prove it. They are ready for retirement. But there is no such thing as spiritual retirement, and our time and place for just "kicking back" spiritually is not now and certainly not here on planet Earth.

You should never feel as though you've already paid your dues, or you've already contributed enough of yourself and your time. There is always more to do, and there is always room to grow. And the greatest days for the Christian are always still ahead! Others are stopped by a very different enemy.

Shame: "I don't deserve to be loved."

Shame shuts down our spiritual progress with guilt. With shame, we feel so guilt-ridden and so unworthy that we are sure God has given up on us. We assume that not even God would want to love us, help us change, or restore our messed-up lives. In some ways shame is the opposite of pride, but it has the same deadly result. Both short-circuit the power of God to fulfill His dreams for us.

When we think in this way, we are fixated on our past, on what we have done, instead of on our future and on what God has done to forgive us. Remember, the apostle Paul said in Philippians 3:13, "Forgetting what lies behind...I press on." If you've had a great year, forget about it or you will be derailed by pride or contentment. If you've had a terrible year that you're ashamed of, forget it or you'll be derailed by shame.

Instead, take Paul's advice and keep reaching forward to the upward call of God in Christ. That's dreaming!

Unbelief: "I really don't believe."

A lack of change in our lives and a failure to dream can indicate that our trust in God is weak or slipping away. We may know intellectually that God promises to do "far more abundantly beyond all that we ask or think," but in our hearts, as indicated in our lack of spiritual initiative, we really don't buy it. We say we believe, but skepticism rules the day. Yet God has always proven Himself to be worthy of trust.

Yes, pressing on and reaching forward is risky business, and risk always requires faith. So at times we will struggle to truly believe God's promises. Yes, we know the facts of our faith, but do we have faith in those same facts? Faith is like a muscle. It grows stronger only when it is stretched beyond its comfort zone. The good news is that God understands our struggle to believe. Be honest with Him; He can handle it!

> THE TRUTH IS, THERE IS NO SAFE REFUGE OUTSIDE OF GOD'S WILL.

Fear: "What will God do?"

Sometimes it is fear that stifles our dreams. We don't trust God with our future. After all, what if God's plan for our lives is different than ours? We worry that we may not share the same dream as He does. It is scary to entrust yourself to another, even when that other is God.

Others of us experience fear that is rooted in the failed aspirations of the past. Past failures make for painful memories, and we don't want to risk a repeat of the pain. Wounds of the past, especially when they result from trusting and being disappointed, are powerful voices in our lives. Perhaps you've had a parent or a loved one walk out on you. Perhaps a family member or friend has let you down, or a spouse has had an affair. People whom you've trusted have betrayed you, and you don't want to be hurt again. Since dreams often involve both risk and faith in God, you opt for the safer status quo.

The truth is, there is no safe refuge outside of God's will— even the status quo can become perilous in the future when it might have been safe in the past. For example, when I was a pastor at my former church, I believed I was doing God's will and pursuing His dreams. The church was healthy and growing. However, after about six years, I felt God leading me to serve Him in Fullerton. Chuck Swindoll, a renowned and gifted author and speaker, had pastored the church in Fullerton for over 20 years. Many of my colleagues jokingly speculated, "Who's the fool that would try and follow Pastor Chuck?" Meanwhile, I was being seriously considered for the job. As I listened to them joke, I thought, *Oh my gosh, I might be the fool. What in the world am I getting myself into?* Moving to Fullerton definitely appeared to be a bigger risk than remaining at my healthy, growing church in Arroyo Grande. However, if God's will was for me to go to Fullerton, then the riskiest move I could have made would have been to stay where I felt secure. One thing I've learned after 11 years in Fullerton (yes, I survived) is that you are safer out on a limb *with God* than you are sitting under the tree *without Him!*

If fear is a problem for you, remember: People may fail you, but God never will. He might work in your life in ways you don't expect and in ways that may feel uncomfortable. But He keeps His promises, and He will never forsake you (Hebrews 13:5).

Frustration: "I've tried, and I'm tired."

If you feel as though you have already tried setting goals with God and failed, take a moment to honestly re-examine your dreams. Ask whether or not you depended upon God or your own best effort. Consider whether or not your dream was what He wanted for you, or one driven by your own aspirations. If you did depend on Him and you really believe your dream is in line with His for your life, then don't give up.

God, like any loving parent, knows how to say no as well as yes. He also understands the importance of timing. "Not right now" is a common response to any child who needs to learn to wait. God may just be working on a different timeline than you had in mind.

And remember, when things seem to be going the "wrong direction," God may be taking you on a "divine detour," since He knows what is "just around the bend" in your life.

Consider the apostle Paul, who was working to build God's church. Next thing you know, he's arrested and thrown into prison—just when his missionary enterprise was exploding with fruitfulness. As the door slammed on his jail cell, it would have been tempting for him to become frustrated and give up his dream of reaching the region for Christ. And he probably did have these thoughts floating around in his head from time to time. However, his imprisonment became a "divine detour" to a far better destination! God slowed him down and took him "off the speaker's circuit" so he could write many of the divinely inspired letters that now, as Scripture, guide the church some 2,000 years later. Wow, what a profitable detour!

> A FAITH-BASED STUBBORN-NESS OF THE SOUL IS A VIRTUE WE ALL NEED.

While there may be a variety of reasons for your frustration, don't let any of them discourage you from dreaming with God and asking, "Okay, Lord, since *that* didn't work…what *next?* How should I adjust the dream? Show me what You want to do now."

When I'm frustrated by delays or unexpected changes in my life, I often sing my own version of the old hymn *Trust and Obey.* You probably know the tune. And here's what I sing:

> Flex and obey,
> For there's no other way,
> To be happy in Jesus,
> But to flex and obey.

Resignation: "Things will never change. I quit."

Some of us have faced many or even all of the above-mentioned dream-killers, and we're ready to give up once and for all. We have resigned ourselves to a life of stasus quo. We go to church yet expect nothing from it. But if you adopt such an attitude, you'll miss out on the joy of letting God transform you while you are here on earth. At the root of resignation is the loss of hope. Hope is such a vital part of keeping dreams alive and continuing to press on that we will spend an entire chapter on nurturing a "sanctified stubbornness" later in the book. Though stubbornness by itself can be a vice, a faith-based stubbornness of the soul is a virtue we all need when we're tempted to say, "I quit."

The Dream God Has for You

So now you're ready to get started and dream new visions of what God can do in you and in your life. How can you envision fresh dreams of what God has for you? What steps can you take to get the process moving?

Get Honest: You Are Not Fine!

First of all, we need to be honest with ourself and admit that we are not fine. I recently read a book titled *TrueFaced,* which plays out a scenario that accurately describes the way many of us live our life:

> Those of us who live in the Land of "Doing Just Fine" are surrounded by nicely scrubbed folk who smile broadly and shake each others' hand firmly. Our conversations go something like this:
>
> "Hi, Milo. How ya doin'?"
>
> "Doin' fine, Mitch. Yourself?"
>
> "Fine, Milo. Fine. Couldn't be finer. Fine day, eh?"
>
> "Fine indeed, Milo. Oh hi, Mildred. How ya doin'?"

"Well, hello, Mitch, I'm doin' fine, considering the circumstances. Just fine. Fine day we're having."

"Yes, it is, Mildred. Fine as fine can be. How's that husband of yours?"

"Well, Mitch, he's doin' fine, too. Whole family's doin' just fine. Can't complain. Yep, I just spoke to Mrs. Sanderson and she told me that she was doing fine, but she had it on reliable information that several other unnamed families were not doing fine. She asked that I not share that publicly, but I tell you, only so you might pray more effectively."

"Well, that's fine with me, Mildred. At least we're fine…just fine."

The time has come for those of us who say we are "Doin' just fine" to acknowledge the truth: We are not fine, not fine at all. We're hurting. We're lonely, confused and frightened.[9]

Many times, the first step forward in awakening our dreams is acknowledging that we're not fine. After all, acknowledging that we are *not* fine is a confession that something needs to change. And great change begins with the right dream. We all have problems, but we know that God can help us, wants to help us, and loves us. Our Savior already knows that we're not fine, He knows all our weaknesses, sins of the heart, and struggles with life. But He also knows grace, gives grace, and frees us to admit we're not fine. So first, get honest. But before the truth bums you out, read on.

Get Grace: In Christ, You Are Already and Always FINEST

On our own, we are never fine. But in Christ, and under His grace, you are already and always the FINEST. Because you are a child of God and Christ lives in you, you can know on any and every day of your life that the following facts are real:

F orgiven and free in Christ
I ndwelt with His Spirit
N ew person in Christ (new heart, new potential)
E ternally secure in His love
S ignificant (purpose to your life)
T ruth you can trust!

In Christ, by His grace, you have the potential to become all that God designed you to be. Now compare God's truth about you to what the world says:

What the World Says to You	The Facts Under Grace
You're guilty and stuck in your past	You're **F**orgiven and free in Christ
You're on your own	You're **I**ndwelt with His Spirit
You're the same old you	You're **N**ew as a person in Christ
You are loved only when you perform	You're **E**ternally secure in His love
You are a cosmic accident	You're **S**ignificant (purpose to your life)
You are unsure about truth	Here's **T**ruth you can trust!

What a glaring contrast between the condemnation of the world and the acceptance of Christ! And His acceptance is not earned, it's a gift. It's grace. There's nothing you can do—even on your worst day—to make God stop loving you. The world's love is selfish, fleeting, and finicky. While you may fall into its favor one day, beware of the next. But God offers a constant and reliable love by grace. This love cannot grow, change, or diminish because it is perfect and has always been perfect. As the apostle Paul declared, "He who began a good work in you will perfect it until the day of Christ Jesus" (Philippians 1:6). The world kills dreams, but grace resurrects them from the dead! Live under grace, as you look to revive your dreams and change.

Get God's Dream…and Pursue It!

So what makes a good dream? How does God want us to dream? Here are some key guidelines to help you as you set goals.

The types of dreams God wants us to pursue will always include the following:

God-centered—The pursuit of God should be the greatest of all our pursuits and, therefore, the first focus of our dreams. Come before Him in prayer and say, "Lord, show me my heart. What can I do next to help nurture my love for Christ? Lord, please deepen my love for You and my appreciation for Your grace. Ground me in Your love." *Set goals for taking your worship and spiritual life* to the next level.

Focused on character—God wants to mold us into the character of our Savior. Therefore holiness, Christlike character, should always show up on your list of dreams. Start with the fruit of the Spirit. Ask God to show you your strengths and weaknesses. "Lord, what do You want me to change as I seek to be more like Jesus? What *character goals* should I set?"

Pursued with a pure heart—David prayed, "Search me, O God, and know my heart" (Psalm 139:23). Since life flows out of the heart, we should always be concerned about the condition of our hearts. God wants to give us new hearts so we can follow Him and obey Him. What *heart issue* should you be working on today?

Faith-based—Your trust and confidence must be in God, not yourself. That will help you focus not only on what is, but on what could be. You will need to trust in the character of your God more than the content of your goals. Sometimes you may miss the target God wanted you to shoot for. Other times you may shoot at the wrong target altogether! Don't let that discourage you from prayerfully, faithfully taking aim at godly goals. Press *forward with faith*, God will be faithful to direct you and work in you.

Word-directed—God's Word defines and directs our dreams with unchanging consistency. If we try to make up our own dreams—without grounding them in Scripture—we run the risk of having ego-driven, pride-driven dreams that will derail us from God's plan. The Bible spells out God's expectations and desires for us, so *allow the Word to direct you* as you dream.

Spirit-led—God uses the Spirit to prompt dreams. In the midst of prayer, the Spirit brings to our mind what God wants to do in our life. He convicts us and guides us. For example, He may prompt you to focus on how to be a better spouse or parent. He may give you a sense of peace about accepting a certain job offer. The Spirit will point to different areas of your life and lead you to make improvements or changes. James says that if we lack wisdom, we can "ask of God, who gives to all generously" (1:5). The Spirit will often use the Word to convict and guide us toward our next dream.

Purpose-driven—Remember that as you dream, you are here on planet Earth for a reason. Jesus said all of life is built on loving God with a passion and loving people as you love yourself. So focus on dreams that *grow your love for God* and *ability to love others*. We'll spend an entire chapter on this at the end of the book. You are also called as a follower of Christ to worship, grow in your faith, serve with your gifts, and reach out to the world. Therefore, expect God to direct you and set goals for each of these vital purposes for your life. Rick Warren's best-selling book *The Purpose Driven Life*[10] is a great place to start rethinking your goals around your God-given purpose.

Focused on vital relationships—Keep in mind that Jesus said the greatest commandment in all of life is a two-part command: love God and love people. So set goals for both. Think through each of the roles God has called you to play in life. Most of us are employed, so set goals for being the *best employee* or employer you can be. Many of us are or will be married. So set goals for being the *best spouse* you can be. Many of us have kids or will have them someday. So set goals for *parenting* in the way you are parented by your heavenly Father. God gives all of us opportunities to touch the lives of friends and neighbors. So make sure you are growing as a friend, a neighbor, a coworker, and certainly at home.

Covered in grace—When you follow dreams that involve God, then you are freed to take risks and guaranteed restoration if you fail. The great Winston Churchill said, "Success is going from failure to failure without losing enthusiasm." And God's grace provides a reason to remain enthusiastic despite disappointments. After all, God is always ready and willing to forgive. With love He turns our apparent failures into important lessons that ultimately lead us to success.

> DON'T MAKE SECONDARY ISSUES SUCH AS HEALTH AND WEALTH THE FOCUS OF YOUR DREAMS.

Pursued with humility and patience—Chase your dreams with humility and patience as you *trust the sovereignty and timing of God.* Remember, change and growth don't happen overnight. Although we live in a world accustomed to instant gratification, spiritual progress is never instant. Expecting instant results will lead to frustration, weariness, and a ready-to-quit attitude. The Christian walk is a lifelong adventure in becoming more and more like Jesus Christ. Make yourself a willing vessel, and God will continue to shape and mold you in His own perfect timing.

Guided by eternal values and priorities—The world encourages dreamers to go for the gold. God calls us to go after things more valuable than gold. The world says, "Look for ways to move up and be in charge." God says, "To be great, look for ways to stoop down and serve." The world says, "The one with the most toys in this life wins." God says, "Be smart and lay up your wealth in heaven. Be generous and rich in good works." The world says, "It's all about you." God says in the Great Commandment, "Life is all about loving God and loving people." So focus on being the best disciple, best husband or wife, best mom or dad, best neighbor and friend you can be.

Seeking God's Vision for You

So as you set goals, dream with God. Ask Him to lead you to one goal or dream for each of the areas mentioned above. It's okay to seek His will and set goals for any aspect of your life. He cares about everything in your life because He cares about you. And don't make secondary issues such as health and wealth the focus of your dreams. The most important dreams are the ones that travel with you no matter where you go and no matter what you do. They make life work whether you are rich or poor, whether you are in good times or bad, whether you are on a roll or you've just been rolled over. To take back your life, focus on what matters, prayerfully get a dream, and go for it!

Now some of you are thinking, *Ok, I know I need to get a dream and chase it. But Dale, I'm too tired to chase anything! My life is overloaded already.*

Don't quit…the next chapter is just for you!

CHOICE #5: **CHASE A BETTER DREAM**

Chapter Summary: Get the Big Idea

Dreams are a powerful force in any life. They get us out of bed in the morning and keep us moving toward a goal. Without them, life gets routine and boring at best. We often suffer from chasing the wrong dreams, the world's empty promises of health, wealth, and happiness. These throw our life out of balance and are never fulfilled. Get started today on redefining your dreams according to God's wisdom for life.

Questions to Guide Discussion and Your Choices

1. We've all wasted time and energy pursuing the wrong dreams. What are some dreams you've pursued, or perhaps even attained, only to be disappointed in the end? In other words, one thing I'm *not* going to worry about in the future is...

2. In light of God's promise to remake you from the inside out, what goals or dreams do you have this year for your spiritual growth? What changes would you like to make in your character as you mature to be more like Christ?

3. The apostle Paul said to forget what lies behind and press onward in Christ. The future *you* in Christ is *not* limited to your past. Name one or two aspects of your past that you need to leave behind so that you are no longer controlled or defined by them.

4. Abiding in and depending on Christ and His Spirit is essential to bringing about real change. What spiritual disciplines will you begin to cultivate or expand upon this year to nurture your dependence on the power of God in your life?

5. Review the list of distractions to dreaming (see pages 100-106). Which ones are hindering you as you try to refocus on fresh dreams for your life?

6. Review the tips for getting started and write down your dreams—God's dreams for your new life in Christ. Use a separate piece of paper and prayerfully write at least one goal for each segment of your life: spiritual, personal, family, work, and ministry.

TAKE BACK YOUR LIFE!

Choice #1: Stop Climbing
Start Down the Ladder to Success

Choice #2: Let God Be God
Build the Ultimate Alliance

Choice #3: Don't Barter with Love—Give It Away
Make Love Your Gift and People Your Priority

Choice #4: Serve Your Way to Success
Nurture a Servant Spirit

Choice #5: Chase a Better Dream
Capture God's Vision for Life

Choice #6: Build a Life-Team
Never Tackle Life Alone

Choice #7: Play to Your Strengths
Stop Trying to Do It All

Choice #8: Improve Your Flex-ability
Be a Lifelong Learner

Choice #9: Slow Down and Focus
Do One Thing at a Time

Choice #10: Nurture Sanctified Stubbornness
Keep the Faith No Matter What

WARNING:
Pride says, "Just go it alone."

TAKE-BACK TIP #6:
Humility says, "Lord, who will go with me?"

CHOICE #6

BUILD A LIFE-TEAM

Never Tackle

Life Alone

In 1989, my family and I packed our station wagon and a big moving truck to move to Southern California. All five of us crammed ourselves and our possessions in the car, on the roof of the car, and in the moving truck. This was a major event for our family. We had never imagined that one day we would move to the West Coast. The possibility of ever moving west had never even entered my mind or my dreams.

At the time, our concept of California had pretty much been shaped by what we saw on television and in the movies—Hollywood, palm trees, swimming pools, beautiful beaches, and some rather unusual individuals. I never thought for a moment that God's next assignment for me would be to serve a church of Californians, let alone become one.

But God knew this move was coming, and as I shut the back of the station wagon, I couldn't help but feel a little bit like a pioneer. The idea of "going west" brought back memories of movies about pioneers who had packed their few precious belongings on a covered wagon and trekked westward with others in a wagon train. In those movies, the pioneers always encountered dangers along the trail. When outlaws or Indians attacked, the trail boss would yell out, "Circle up!" And the wagons would form a circle to help protect everyone.

However, somewhere along the journey, usually one family would have a falling out with the trail boss and thus would attempt to strike out on their own. With the Wild West being the dangerous place it was, inevitably animals or other enemies would prey on these stragglers. Their wagon would be set on fire or shot full of bullets or arrows. Most of the family would be taken captive or suffer a horrible death. Of course, to elevate the suspense of the movie, one survivor would always manage to sneak away into the bushes and live to tell the story to others. The family had started the journey in pursuit of a dream, only to have it turn into a nightmare.

These movies clearly taught a lesson for life: When you set out to pursue your dream, never travel alone. Whether going east or west, life on planet Earth has many dangers, and we have an enemy who wants to discourage us, damage us, or destroy our faith at every opportunity. When we are alone, we are easy targets. But if we travel with a team of others, we can "circle up" and fend off Satan's attacks.

Pride Leads to Isolation

How does all this relate to our climb down the ladder to success? Humility reminds us that we all need help. Life is a team sport. Pride tempts us to prove ourselves and do everything on our own. Humility, by contrast, sees the wisdom of working together with others. So the next step down the ladder is all about *team*.

Pride says, "Just go it alone."

Pride says, "I don't need anyone else's help." In the Bible, we don't have to go very far to see the first incident of this kind of defiance. It appears in Genesis chapter 3. Pride compelled Adam and Eve to eat the forbidden fruit because they wanted to be like God. Let's read what happened:

> *The eyes of both of them were opened, and they knew that they were naked; and they sewed fig leaves together and made themselves loin coverings. They heard the sound of the LORD God walking in the garden in the cool of the day, and the man and his wife hid themselves from the presence of the LORD God among the trees of the garden. Then the LORD God called to the man, and said to him, "Where are you?" [Adam] said, "I heard the sound of You in the garden, and I was afraid because I was naked; so I hid myself." And [God] said, "Who told you that you were naked? Have you eaten from the tree of which I commanded you not to eat?" The man said, "The woman whom You gave to be with me, she gave me from the tree, and I ate." Then the LORD God said to the woman, "What is this you have done?" And the woman said, "The serpent deceived me, and I ate"*
> *(verses 7–13).*

What do we learn from this? Ever since the fall, we have responded to our sin, our weaknesses, our insufficiency in three ways. Adam and Eve model all of them for us. First, we feel ashamed and hide or *isolate* ourselves because we recognize we are not all that God made us to be. Second, we declare our *independence* and try to deny or cover up the problem. Back then, Adam and Eve sewed together leaves; today, we wear masks by pretending that we are fine. And third, we express *indignation* and blame others for our mistakes—in the same way that Adam blamed Eve for offering him the fruit and God for making this woman in the first place! In summary, we react in these ways:

- *Isolation*—in shame we distance ourselves from God and others.

- *Independence*—in pride we deny the problem and try to fix it on our own.

- *Indignation*—we become defensive, dodge responsibility, and blame others.

The Importance of a Life-Team

HEROES OFTEN GET THE HEADLINES, BUT BEHIND EVERY TRIUMPH IS A TEAM.

Because life on planet Earth is always dangerous, we need one another. Many of us refuse to admit our need. Our world exalts those who act tough and independent. It idolizes the self-made and considers humility a weakness. The fact is, humility and the teamwork that flow from it is the way life was meant to be lived. It is not weakness but wisdom to embrace this vital fact of life. People seldom, if ever, accomplish great things alone. Heroes often get the headlines, but behind every triumph is a team. It's true for all of life. You need a life-team to play the game well and win.

> *Humility says, "Lord, who will go with me?"*

Proverbs 19:20 says, "Listen to counsel and accept discipline, that you may be wise the rest of your days." To admit that you need help does not signify weakness, but wisdom. Remember our example of the wagon train? The prideful pioneer who took off alone was not showing strength but ignorance! He was putting his own life—and the lives of his family—at risk.

God created us to need help. This fact of life is evident from the beginning of creation. In Genesis 2:18, God said, "It is not good for the man to be alone; I will make him a helper suitable for him." Notice that God made this observation *before* humanity's fall into sin. The world was still perfect, and so was Adam. God had looked at all that He had made, and said it was good. But there was one thing God saw that *wasn't* good—Adam was alone. God knew he needed help. Adam and Eve needed each other. This is life as it was meant to be.

Though our need for help appeared *before* the fall, the need became heightened *after* the fall. Hebrews 3:12-13 says,

> *Take care, brethren, that there not be in any one of you an evil, unbelieving heart that falls away from the living God. But encourage one another day after day, as long as it is still called "Today," so that none of you will be hardened by the deceitfulness of sin.*

The deceitfulness and misleading nature of sin heightens our need for the wisdom of others. We all need to help each other navigate the journey called life.

Have you ever noticed that the two greatest commandments in the Bible reflect our need for help and relationships with others? Jesus said in Matthew 22:37-39,

> *"You shall love the Lord your God with all your heart, and with all your soul, and with all your mind." This is the great and foremost commandment. The second is like it, "You shall love your neighbor as yourself." On these two commandments depend the whole Law and the Prophets.*

We all need God and godly friends. We were created to depend on these relationships. But this does not mean God created us with a deficiency; rather, this need actually contributes to our reflection of the image of God. God is three-in-one; He is

IF YOU WANT TO EXPERIENCE THE LOVE OF GOD...YOU MUST CONNECT TO THE PEOPLE OF GOD.

the Trinity. Thus, by nature, He is a relational being.

Jesus further emphasized relationships in John 13:34: "A new commandment I give to you, that you love one another, even as I have loved you, that you also love one another." The timing of this command is significant. Jesus knew He was about to die. He gathered the disciples and told them that He was going to suffer and die. Thus, this command was given to let them know that they would survive after He was gone by loving each other. Jesus Christ would still love them, but He would deliver His love through them. Like it or not, we who are Christians are the delivery system for the love of God.

Our Need for Others

Some time ago a man came to my office for counseling. He was frustrated because he did not feel God's love or presence in his life. He had felt it in the past, as a young man in our high school and college ministries, but no longer. He had prayed for it, and as far as he was concerned, it hadn't come. He was tempted to give up on God and walk away from the faith. He couldn't understand why God, if He was alive and cared, wouldn't reach out to him.

I just sat and listened. Then a thought came to me. I told him that the very fact that I was there listening to him, caring about him, was the love of God in action. If it weren't for God's love, I wouldn't even care about his youthful doubts and questions. I would have been preoccupied with other "more important" things to do than to sit and listen to him. But Christ was alive, living in me, listening through me, and eager to answer his questions with love. I asked him if he sensed that I really cared. He did. I told him that what he was feeling was not just the love of Dale but the love of God in me for him. You see, if you want to experience the love of God, the wisdom of God, and the comfort of God, you must connect to the people of God, His church, the body of Christ. God loves through us, period. That is His plan.

As the young man recounted his struggle with faith, he realized he had slowly disconnected from his friends at church, from ministry to others, and from trips to serve Christ and the poor. He remembered that his greatest times of intimacy with God were times spent with God's people doing God's business. He remembered sensing the presence of God as he shared his faith, served the poor, and helped a friend in need. In short, he realized that God had not moved, but instead, he himself had moved. As the man reengaged with the life of the church, he reconnected with the life and the love of God.

In the church, every believer is both needed and needy. In 1 Corinthians 12:7, Paul wrote, "To each one is given the manifestation of the Spirit for the common good." In context, this passage is talking about spiritual gifts. God gives each of us special gifts, and though you might not feel like it, others in the church need you and your giftedness. God grants us these gifts for the purpose of building up one another "for the common good." Later in that same passage, Paul compares us believers to the various parts of the human body and writes, "The eye cannot say to the hand, 'I have no need of you'" (verse 21). God created everyone in the body of Christ such that we all need each other.

Life is a team sport, and to live a great life requires great teams in every area of your life. In the corporate world, a leader is only as good as the team he or she builds around him or her. In your marriage, you will be effective only if you work as a team with your spouse. In parenting, you want to build a team with your spouse, your kids, and the youth ministry at your church. Depend on others' gifts for areas in which you are not so gifted. This is not a strategy of the weak, but of the wise.

The apostle Paul was one of the greatest Christians in the

New Testament era, but he was not too great to realize the value of a good team. He wasn't a solitary pioneer taking on the world like the Lone Ranger. He knew that even the Lone Ranger had a sidekick named Tonto. All through Romans chapter 16, Paul names individuals and teams who worked together with him. For example, he says, "Greet Prisca and Aquila, my fellow workers in Christ Jesus, who for my life risked their own necks" (verses 3-4). Prisca and Aquila made up a team willing to put their lives on the line for Paul. Having that kind of support gave Paul a real advantage in a dangerous world.

The Advantage of a Life-Team

The Bible clearly outlines the advantages of working together with a team. Ecclesiastes 4:9-12 affirms the teamwork strategy:

> *Two are better than one because they have*
> *a good return for their labor. For if either of*
> *them falls, the one will lift up his companion.*
> *But woe to the one who falls when there is not*
> *another to lift him up. Furthermore, if two lie*
> *down together they keep warm, but how can*
> *one be warm alone? And if one can overpower*
> *him who is alone, two can resist him. A cord of*
> *three strands is not quickly torn apart.*

Notice that the passage mentions not one but several advantages of teams, as detailed in the chart below.

Alone, life will be...	*But together, we can...*
hard	get a greater return
hurtful	pick up one another
cold	warm one another
dangerous	defend one another
demanding	strengthen one another

We could easily spend a whole chapter taking a closer look at this passage, but the most important point to remember is this: You will get a lot farther in life with a team than by yourself. If you want to accomplish more, be picked up when you fall, be warmed when you're cold, be defended when you're attacked, and be strengthened when you feel weak, link up with a team for life. While the bulk of the passage seems to be referring to a team of two, the last line expands it: "A cord of three strands is not quickly torn apart." Don't forget that regardless of how many people your team incorporates, the most important player of all is God. He is that third strand, invisible but real.

The Developing of a Life-Team

How do we get started in building a team? I believe the highest priority is to develop what I call the home-court advantage. In sports, teams always play better at home than they do on the road. As you strengthen your relationships at home, your relationships elsewhere will improve as well.

Parents and Children

Ephesians 6:1-3 says, "Children, obey your parents in the Lord, for this is right. Honor your father and mother (which is the first commandment with a promise), so that it may be well with you, and that you may live long on the earth." Do you who are children want to have a better and longer life? Then learn to relate well with your parents. Listen to them, learn from them, and submit to them, even when they drive you up the wall. Why? Because it is great preparation for life. You will gain invaluable wisdom and experience that will equip you for survival in the real world. You see, in the real world, you will work for people who will, at times, drive you up the wall. You will have to work with coworkers who at times "just don't get it." You may find yourself leading a company or organization through change that feels to them like your kids' favorite music group! Training in team building and relationships begins right out of the womb. So no matter what your age, practice on your parents. This first relationship sets the tone for every relationship in your life.

If you get upset with your parents and lash out at them, and that becomes a habit, eventually you're going to act the same toward others—your spouse, your friends, and even your boss at work. And if that happens, you will end up divorced or unemployed. I don't know if this is a completely universal truth, but I have always told my daughters that the way a man treats his mother is a forecast of the way he will someday treat his wife. When children learn how to communicate with their parents, especially in times of conflict, they gain skills that will help them negotiate conflict effectively when it arises in their marriage or their workplace. Most important of all, learning to listen to and submit to our parents trains us to do the same with our heavenly Father, the ultimate authority figure. If you want to enjoy healthy relationships with others, including God, you need to start by building a healthy relationship with your parents.

Husbands and Wives

Likewise, if you cannot get along with your spouse, surviving in the outside world is going to be that much harder. After all, your spouse is supposed to be your number-one supporter and team member. A spouse may put up with your idiosyncrasies for a time, but the world will not. So learn to excel in your marriage, and you will increase your odds for success in every arena of life. In the church, we often talk about the need for accountability among believers so that they can remain spiritually healthy and grow to maturity. The marriage relationship is a special, God-designed accountability group. When you build a strong marriage, you gain a partner for life like no other on earth. To take back your life, start at home and build a team.

Close Friends

Whether you are single or married, having a few good friends who will risk their necks for you can contribute immensely to your home-court advantage. Proverbs 27:17 says, "Iron sharpens iron, so one man sharpens another." Find a few faithful friends—friends who share your faith and values. One definition describes a team as "a group of players on the same side in a game."[11] That's what we all need—a few people who are on our side and who will fight for us. A definition of the word *teamwork* reads, "a cooperative effort to achieve a common goal."[12] Put these definitions together and you come up with faithful friends who will fight for you and for the life God has called you to live. Together, we can help one another take back our life and keep it under control. Together, we can climb down the ladder to success, ready to help catch one another if we begin to stumble or fall.

> FINDING FAITHFUL FRIENDS STARTS WITH BEING A SERVANT.

Finding Faithful Friends

Truly faithful friends are hard to find. However, they do exist, and here is my advice on how to find them: become one yourself. In other words, be the kind of person others would want to team up with. You can't change other people, but you can definitely change yourself. As you make these changes, others who value the same things will be attracted to you. When you start loving other people in this way, they will begin loving you in return. Be humble and take the first step by being what you want others to be.

Finding faithful friends starts with being a servant. Be gracious to others, quick to forgive and accept. Be honest, telling the truth with gentleness. Be devoted, sticking with people that life puts on your team whether you choose them or not. Be ready to bear with them, too. We all have our problems, and from time to time, others will need to put up with us. So be ready to be patient. We also need to submit to one another and accept one another.

We need to learn to comfort, encourage, and rejoice with one another in both the good times and the bad.

As you become this kind of person, other people of like mind will surface and be drawn to you. You'll find one another, and you'll start pursuing your dreams together. And finally you will be ready to head "out West" like those pioneers, ready and willing to pull together until the journey is over. Remember, great things are never accomplished alone. Think *team* to take back your life.

CHOICE #6: BUILD A LIFE-TEAM

Chapter Summary: Get the Big Idea

Life really was designed, from creation, to be a team sport. No one can go it alone and still experience the joy of life as it is meant to be lived. We all need help. We all need a team of friends and family who can travel with us and tackle life together. You are both needy and needed by others. So stop, reflect, and ask God to help you assemble a world-class team for life!

Questions to Guide Discussion and Your Choices

1. Most of us have been raised to value independence and self-reliance. What influences in your life have encouraged too much of a prideful independence and an unwillingness to ask for help when you need it?

2. Review the advantages of a life-team as stated in the discussion about Ecclesiastes 4:9-12. Which of these advantages appeal to you? When in your life have you experienced the blessing of being supported by others? Where have you missed it?

3. Teams are effective only when the members know each other and grow to love and trust one another. And that requires regular time together. How do you plan to alter your life to make time for building these close friendships?

4. Life-teams start at home. How can you better share the load with your spouse (friends or roommates, if you're single)? What is your plan for strengthening your life-team?

5. Life-teams need close friendships. Can you think of one or two friends you can truly depend on? If not, ask God to lead you to a couple new friends, and start nurturing those relationships through time spent together.

6. Life-teams need faithful and full-of-faith friends. You need to surround yourself with a few friends who share your commitment to Christ and His Word. Who are they? When and where will you connect so you can support one another? Start today, and ask them to help you take back your life!

TAKE BACK YOUR LIFE!

Choice #1: Stop Climbing
Start Down the Ladder to Success

Choice #2: Let God Be God
Build the Ultimate Alliance

Choice #3: Don't Barter with Love—Give It Away
Make Love Your Gift and People Your Priority

Choice #4: Serve Your Way to Success
Nurture a Servant Spirit

Choice #5: Chase a Better Dream
Capture God's Vision for Life

Choice #6: Build a Life-Team
Never Tackle Life Alone

Choice #7: Play to Your Strengths
Stop Trying to Do It All

Choice #8: Improve Your Flex-ability
Be a Lifelong Learner

Choice #9: Slow Down and Focus
Do One Thing at a Time

Choice #10: Nurture Sanctified Stubbornness
Keep the Faith No Matter What

WARNING:
*Pride says, "I'm God's
gift to humanity."*

TAKE-BACK TIP #7:
*Humility says, "What has
God given me for humanity?"*

PLAY TO YOUR STRENGTHS

Stop Trying to Do It All

Psalm 23 is one of the most frequently quoted and memorized psalms in the Bible. There, King David describes what life is like under the care of our Lord, who is the ultimate Great Shepherd. As we read this psalm, we can easily picture in our minds a quiet, serene, and restful life—the kind we would all like to have, life as it was meant to be. Read it slowly and see if it doesn't appeal to you:

> *The LORD is my shepherd,*
> *I shall not want.*
> *He makes me lie down in green pastures;*
> *He leads me beside quiet waters.*
> *He restores my soul;*
> *He guides me in the paths of righteousness*
> *For His name's sake.*

> *Even though I walk through the valley of the*
> *   shadow of death,*
> *I fear no evil, for You are with me;*
> *Your rod and Your staff, they comfort me.*
> *You prepare a table before me in the presence of my*
> *   enemies;*
> *You have anointed my head with oil;*
> *My cup overflows.*
> *Surely goodness and lovingkindness will follow me*
> *   all the days of my life,*
> *And I will dwell in the house of the LORD forever.*

I shall not want...I can be content, satisfied, and happy with life just as it is. Lying down in green pastures, by quiet waters...I can rest in the promise of plenty to eat and drink with no one hassling me to get more done. He restores my soul...instead of being frustrated and tired I can be refreshed, relaxed, and ready for whatever comes my way. I fear no evil...I do not need to fear anything or anyone, but rather can have confidence that my Shepherd has it all under control. And as for the future? Surely goodness and mercy will follow me all the days of my life...I have no reason to worry, or be concerned, even if my IRA or 401(k) disappears tomorrow! Doesn't that sound appealing? But if you're like most of us, your life sounds more like something out of "Psalm 23, the Antithesis," which was written by Marsha Hornok, the wife of a friend of mine in seminary:

> *The clock is my dictator, I shall not rest.*
> *It makes me lie down only when exhausted.*
> *It leads me to deep depression.*
> *It hounds my soul.*
> *It leads me in circles of frenzy for activities' sake.*
> *Even though I run frantically from task to task,*
> *I will never get it all done, for my ideal is with me.*
> *Deadlines and my need for approval, they drive me.*

*They demand my performance from me beyond the
     limits of my schedule.*
*They anoint my head with migraines, and my in-
     basket overfloweth.*
*Surely fatigue and time pressure will follow me all
     the days of my life,*
*And I will dwell in the bonds of frustration forever
     and ever. Amen.*[13]

Does that sound more like reality, more like life out of control? Most of us have more responsibilities than we can handle, with not a moment to spare for lying by still waters except for an occasional trip to the beach. And even that isn't necessarily restful when you have to fight traffic, load and unload the car, keep your eyes on the kids, and more.

Simplifying Your Life

As we continue discovering how we can take our life back—how we can get back to life as it's meant to be—one key essential is that we somehow simplify our life. We need to slow ourselves down and figure out a way to accomplish more while doing less. Pride tells us to never admit that we can't do it all, so we just try to work harder and faster. Once again, humility and the wisdom of God has a better approach:

Admit we can't do it all.
Ask for help and build a life-team.
*Then focus on doing less of whatever, and more of
     our best stuff.*
In a word, specialize.
Play to your strengths and stop trying to do it all!

In the last chapter we learned that life is designed by God to be lived as a team sport. But we tend to live it as if it's a time trial, just ourselves racing against the clock. If life is a team sport, then it only makes sense that you should focus most of your time on doing what you do best. God wants you to maximize your personal gifts and abilities for the good of the team.

A Review of the First Five Choices

Now before I explain how we can do that, it's important for us to review our God-given strategy for taking back our life. Each step is sequential, and we need to remember the previous steps so we can better understand how the current step fits in the big picture.

First, recognize that life is out of control because you were headed in the wrong direction. *Stop climbing* the ladder...and change direction. Real life as it was meant to be is found down the ladder, humbly walking with God, not climbing after worldly success without Him.

Next, choose to *let God be God.* Surrender control of your life to Christ, the omni-everything who is much wiser. It just makes sense for us to get beyond our pride and admit our need for help. We need to let Christ take full control—that's real wisdom.

Third, choose to *love others* and *make people your priority.* Love others with God's kind of love, and don't expect anything in return. This will transform your relationships and spice up your life!

Fourth, choose to *serve your way to success.* We can choose to serve as a lifestyle. In fact, serving is the key to real success. When you nurture a servant mind-set in every relationship, at home and at work, every day of your life will improve. Live to give, not to get, and see what happens!

The fifth new choice we need to make is to *start chasing new dreams*—God's dreams instead of the world's dreams, which later turn into nightmares. We have a big God who has big plans for us, and we ought to *imagine* what God can and will do in and through us. Begin prayerfully setting goals in line with life as it's meant to be and go for it! Simply clarifying our goals and asking God to go to work on us is half the battle.

But sixth, as we pursue new goals, we shouldn't go about them alone. *Build a life-team* with family members and friends who share your vision and values. In Scripture, these fellow disciples of Jesus are called "the body of Christ." Christ promises to help you, and He does so through His body on planet Earth as well as through His indwelling Spirit and His Word. We're all members of one body, and we all need one another.

Focus Down—Play to Your Strengths

That brings us to our next point: If I'm part of a team pursuing the dreams God has given me, what is my role? Where do I fit in? And how can I make sure I don't repeat the mistake of trying to do too much all at once? That's what *specializing* is all about. Play to your strengths, and quit trying to do it all.

> PLAY TO YOUR STRENGTHS, AND QUIT TRYING TO DO IT ALL.

Pride—"I'm God's gift to humanity."

Pride says, "I've got to do it all!" It produces a driven, "got to" lifestyle. It says, "I've got to do this…I've got to do that…I've got to do everything!" This person feels like he or she needs to climb higher and faster on the ladder to success. What causes this type of thinking? Our Monster, My Life, is fueled by three "gottas."

I've Gotta Please Everyone

Many of us, when we were growing up, were taught that it's essential to make everyone around us happy. We were told to please our parents, teachers, bosses, fellow church members, pastors, friends, neighbors, and more. Now there's nothing wrong with showing love for people and helping them. Jesus Himself said that the secret to a great life is serving others. But we have to be realistic about what we can and can't do. There's a difference between a simple desire to please people whenever possible and a driven compulsion that we must please everyone at all times.

I've Gotta Impress Everyone

To what extent are you concerned about your image to others? There's nothing wrong with taking care of your appearance and putting your best foot forward. I'm sure Jesus did whatever was appropriate for the sake of representing His Father in an honorable way. But we can be certain He didn't feel compelled to impress people. In fact, we know there were many people who were not impressed with Him, and He was comfortable with that. He didn't worry about people's opinions. He was a God-pleaser, not a man-pleaser. Realizing you have nothing to prove, no one to impress, is a great step forward as you try to take back your life.

I've Gotta Achieve Something

It's okay to have goals and dreams in our lives. All of us should strive to do our best on the job, at school, in our homes. But there's a difference between having a dream and feeling like you must accomplish something in order to feel good about yourself or be accepted. As you go after that dream, ask yourself: Am I putting pressure on myself to achieve this goal to affirm my value? Is my self-worth based in my accomplishments or in what God has accomplished in making me His child?

Breaking Free from the "Gottas"

When the "gottas" start driving the way you plan your day, then you have lost control and you are at their mercy. You'll find yourself doing things that undermine life as it's meant to be. You will sacrifice the important for the urgency of the "gottas" and suffer for it. You'll do something stupid and then wonder out loud, "Why in the world did I do that?" The three "gottas" we just reviewed are quiet but powerful forces in our lives.

God wants to free you from the "gottas" and replace them with grace. Grace and its Lord whisper, "Relax. You don't have to please everyone—just Me. You don't have to impress people; just focus on being what I created you to be. I will always love you as My child, and My love is not based on your performance. Relax."

> *Humility says—"What has God given me for humanity?"*

The Less-Is-More Approach

Humility takes the less-is-more approach and says, "Lord, I can't do it all, so what do You want me to do today?" We need to get into the habit of starting each day by asking, "Lord, what *should* I do?" In other words, we need to take inventory right from the start, lift everything up to the Lord, and ask Him for wisdom to choose when we can't do it all. Only then can we silence those persistent "gottas" that keep driving us to take on more than we can handle. Instead of saying, "I've got to please *everyone*, impress *someone*, achieve *something*," we need to live by a simpler but more significant set of desires:

> THE SECRET TO LIFE IN TODAY'S COMPLEX WORLD IS TO SIMPLY LIVE TO PLEASE ONE.

I Want to Please One

It's okay to care about people, but don't live to please them. Jesus once said, "No one can serve two masters; for either he will hate the one and love the other, or he will be devoted to one and despise the other" (Matthew 6:24). Multiple bosses will drive anyone crazy. The secret to life in today's complex world is to simply live to please One, your heavenly Father. Now that doesn't change the fact that I have multiple people in my life who all want and need a piece of me. But it anchors my life and my choices around one preeminent Lord and Life-Master. When I focus on pleasing Him, He will guide me as I seek to serve my spouse, my kids, my church, and my boss. Only He is smart enough to pull all that off!

Now the good news is that my God understands the real needs of the others in my life. So as I serve and listen to and follow God, He will indeed watch out for my wife, my kids, and even my boss at work. He will help make me a better servant of all without driving me to live to please them all. That's simplification.

I Need to Impress No One

As a child of God, you are already loved and accepted. While it's good to offer your best at whatever you do, don't take on additional responsibilities simply because you're afraid that to decline them will hurt your reputation in other people's eyes. Jesus knew some people weren't pleased with Him, but He didn't waste time trying to convince them otherwise. He lived for His Father's approval, not the approval of people. If you live to please the Father, you'll know true satisfaction within you. But if you live to please people, you'll always struggle because you'll never be able to make everyone happy.

I'm Then Free to Serve Others as a Gift out of My Giftedness

Once you free yourself from the "gottas," then you become free to serve others out of a heart that wants to give, with no strings attached. Jesus Himself illustrated this in John chapter 13:

> *Before the Feast of the Passover, Jesus knowing*
> *that His hour had come that He would depart*
> *out of this world to the Father, having loved*
> *His own who were in the world, He loved them*
> *to the end.... [Jesus] got up from supper, and*
> *laid aside His garments; and taking a towel,*
> *He girded Himself. Then He poured water into*
> *the basin, and began to wash the disciples' feet*
> *(verses 1,4-5).*

Here we see Jesus ready to depart from this world. He had completed the work the Father had given to Him. And right to the end, He remained a servant and did exactly what His Father called Him to do. He was also free to show His love to the disciples by washing their feet. In His years of ministry, Jesus didn't get bogged down by extra projects others could have done. And He didn't serve merely for the sake of pleasing or impressing people.

One of the major hindrances we face when it comes to serving in the church is the compulsion within us to impress people. Beware when that's your motive. We shouldn't seek our sense of fulfillment or purpose in the things we do. We already have all the love and acceptance we need by virtue of the fact we are children of the living God. We are forgiven, indwelt by the Spirit, and eternally significant and secure. That should free us from any need to impress others.

NONE OF US IS MEANT TO BE A DO-IT-ALL GENERALIST.

Explore Your God-Given Uniqueness

Here are four tips to free you from the "gottas." First, realize *you are a unique creation of God.* He made you different from everyone else. Every believer has unique gifts he or she can contribute in service of others. None of us is meant to be a do-it-all generalist. Rather, each of us has special functions that are designed to complement one another. The apostle Paul addressed this in Romans chapter 12, which begins with a word about surrendering ourselves: "I urge you, brethren, by the mercies of God, to present your bodies a living and holy sacrifice, acceptable to God, which is your spiritual service of worship" (verse 1). From there, Paul goes on and exhorts us to play from our strengths. Listen to God's approach to discovering and deploying them:

Be Humble—"Through the grace given to me I say to everyone among you not to think more highly of himself than he ought to think" (verse 3). While you're a wonderfully gifted person, don't start thinking too much of yourself. Be careful about becoming prideful. Remember that all our gifts are from God.

Be Wise—"Think so as to have sound judgement" (verse 3). That is, have sound judgment about yourself. Paul isn't saying we're to have a low view of ourselves. Rather, we are to be honest about our strengths and weaknesses. We should know what we can and can't do. We're all different, and that's the way God designed us.

Be Unique—"As God has allotted to each a measure of faith" (verse 3). God has given to each of us different measures and expressions of faith. Every one of us will serve in different ways. Get to know yourself and celebrate who God has made you to be. Don't ever wish you were someone or something else. God made you unique for a reason. You are of value to Him and to others. As a T-shirt I once saw said, "God don't make no junk."

Be Appreciative—"Just as we have many members in one body and all the members do not have the same function, so we, who are many, are one body in Christ, and individually members one of another. Since we have gifts that differ according to the grace given to us" (verses 4-6). We're all different; we "do not have the same function." We are gifted in ways that enable us to do specific tasks within the church. And if we're all using our various gifts, everyone's needs will be met. There's no need for any one of us to attempt to do everything on our own. Remember, life is a team sport.

Be Focused—"Each of us is to exercise them accordingly" (verse 6). We're to stay focused and to serve according to our strengths. We're to focus on maximizing the gift or gifts God has entrusted to us. As verses 6-8 say, if service is our gift, then serve on! If teaching is our gift, then teach well. If leadership is our unique strength, then lead with diligence...and so on. As we get focused and spend more and more time doing what we do best, life comes back under control. We can make more of a difference in much less time. Less is more. This is life as it's meant to be: A world of gifted people serving one another for the common good. You are unique for a reason. So play from your strengths, and do so with humility.

Here's a second tip:

Trust and Share the Load

When we read about the early church in the book of Acts, we find that the reason the people functioned so well was because they trusted one another and worked together as a team. A wonderful example of this appears in Acts 6:1-7. There, we read that some widows were not receiving adequate care. The apostles were very busy and were unable to care for these widows. So the apostles mobilized a special group and empowered them to tackle the problem—and as a result, the widows' needs were met. Notice the apostles remained focused on what they were uniquely gifted and called to do—pray and teach the Word. They didn't try to oversee every part of church life. Rather, they trusted others with certain responsibilities and saw the value of teamwork. As a result, the needs were met, unity was preserved, and the movement attracted more people. And so the church continued to grow.

What happened in Acts 6:1-7 is a great snapshot of how we should handle all of life. No matter what our role—whether we are managing a home or Homeland Security—we will always be faced with more demands than we can handle. And we will have to be willing to give up control, trust others, and work together as a team. If we try to micromanage everything in our life and hold all of life tightly, we'll end up with no life at all.

Now, when it comes to focusing on our strengths, we probably won't be able to make the necessary changes overnight. Entrusting responsibilities to other people usually requires that we coach and encourage them. We have to train and equip them, and that takes work. But eventually you will get to the point where the other person can do the job as well as you, or even better. Just make sure you let it go! Then life will become a little more manageable. You'll have simplified your life and enriched someone else's life as they now put their strengths into play. This is true in the church, in the workplace, and in the home.

So what's the third tip?

Serve from Your Optimum Capabilities

If you want to be the very best man, woman, or child that you can be, and if you want to achieve as much as God desires for you to achieve, then it's vital that you focus on serving in your areas of unique giftedness and not attempt to do everything. This dovetails nicely with what Paul said in 1 Corinthians 12:4-7:

> *Now there are varieties of gifts, but the same*
> *Spirit. And there are varieties of ministries,*
> *and the same Lord. There are varieties of effects,*
> *but the same God who works all things in all*
> *persons. But to each one is given the manifesta-*
> *tion of the Spirit for the common good.*

There are varieties of gifts and ministries, and each one of us is "given the manifestation"—in other words, we are uniquely gifted—"for the common good."

GOD CAN USE EVERYTHING ABOUT YOU TO TOUCH OTHER PEOPLE'S LIVES IN WAYS THAT NO ONE ELSE CAN.

And not only are you uniquely gifted by God, but you also have specific passions and experiences that determine your special place in the body of Christ. Everything you experience in life—painful or pleasurable—affects you, changes you, and equips you to help other people. God can use everything about you to touch other people's lives in ways that no one else can, which is why every single one of us has great value to God's work here on earth.

You might be thinking, *I'm not sure what my gifts and passions are.* If that's the case, that's okay. But don't use that as an excuse to stay uninvolved. The best way to find out how God can use you is to pick an area of ministry that appeals to you and sign up. Explore the options before you. As you do, you'll get a better sense of your strengths and weaknesses. You'll see whether you have a natural giftedness for a particular area of ministry. You passions will surface. Along the way, be sure to ask God for guidance. Ask Him to nudge you in the right direction and to bring along people who can help you determine your area of unique giftedness. Then serve with your best stuff, both inside and outside the church.

In summary, here's how you can discover your area of giftedness:

- walk with God in humility
- serve faithfully
- pray and ask for direction
- study and evaluate your gifts and passions
- ask, Where and how has God used me so far?
- shift more of your time towards your areas of giftedness and passion

Develop and Build on Your Strengths

Finally, keep in mind that discovering and developing your unique giftedness is a lifelong process. As you find your niche in life, your career or your ministry, you will want to build on your strengths and keep developing them. Paul encouraged Timothy in that manner when he said, "I remind you to kindle afresh the gift of God which is in you" (2 Timothy 1:6). Paul wanted to make sure Timothy didn't let his gift become dormant or underutilized. And as you develop your strengths, remember to let go of your weaknesses.

Great lives are never built by improving our weaknesses, but by maximizing our strengths.

There's another problem that often arises as time goes on: As we grow in using our area of giftedness, we sometimes become involved in more and more activities to the point that we're back in square one again. We return to being overloaded, overworked, and overwhelmed. How can we keep that from happening?

Here's a diagram you might find helpful as you determine your priorities. I use this in my "How to Lead & Still Have a Life" seminars to help people figure out what they should and shouldn't be doing. Every person has certain gifts, passions, and experiences. These make you who you are and enrich your abilities. The zone where these three gifts overlap is your zone of "optimum capabilities." It is where your time is invested with the greatest return. It is where you provide optimum value to others. It is, in short, your best stuff!

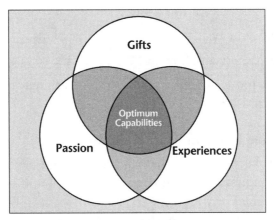

You want to serve as much as possible in the zone where the three circles overlap. Do the things you're great at. Don't allow yourself to be tempted to do every little thing that comes your way…or you'll find yourself becoming too busy again. Be a specialist, and not a jack of all trades. Learn to just say no! Let go of what you're not good at. Over time, as the following diagram illustrates, you'll want to move more of your time and energy (the arrow in the circle) toward your optimum capabilities, where your gifts, passions, and experiences overlap.

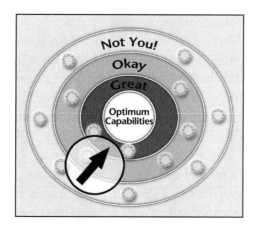

The Way to Finish Strong

There's a wonderful encouragement the apostle Paul gave to Timothy in 2 Timothy 4:5: "Endure hardship, do the work of an evangelist, fulfill your ministry." Notice the three key phrases in that statement:

Endure—Life isn't easy; it can get messy. But hang in there. Don't give up. Keep focusing on your unique calling and go for it!

Do the work—Doing your job well will require effort. That's why it's so essential you focus on your strengths. It's better that you do a few tasks well rather than many tasks poorly.

> THE DIFFERENCE BETWEEN A RIVER AND A SWAMP IS FOCUS.

Fulfill your ministry—Do *your* ministry, not that which can and should be done by others. Fulfill what God has put on *your* heart, and do it well—all the way to the end of your life. Make it your mission to be able to say, "I finished strong."

When you live with focus, serving others from your strengths, life gets exciting. Your impact goes up and your sense of busyness goes down. You accomplish more on less. You stop spreading yourself too thin and experience a sense of real accomplishment. You are now making a difference and having an impact.

It's been said that the difference between a river and a swamp is focus. A river has a narrow, deep channel that focuses the force of the stream and carries things forward. It gets you to your destination. It brings life and makes a difference.

A swamp, while it can have just as much water as a river, lacks a well-defined channel. It is a shallow body of water going nowhere. It covers a lot of ground, but it stagnates and stinks. It breeds disease and death.

Which do you want to be? Be like a river—make a differnce—focus down and play to your strengths!

CHOICE #7: PLAY TO YOUR STRENGTHS

Chapter Summary: Get the Big Idea
You are a uniquely created child of God. Every follower of Christ is blessed with certain gifts, passions, and experiences that make you who you are. Like great athletes, we all need to specialize as much as possible. You will get more done on less time and energy, and with more joy, when you play from your God-given strengths. Get started, and see how fun life can be!

Questions to Guide Discussion and Your Choices
1. Review the three "gottas" in the beginning of the chapter. Which of these tend to drive you to accomplish too much by yourself and overload your life?

2. How does the less-is-more approach to life simplify and lower the pressure on your life? Think of one area in your life in which you plan to put this into practice right away.

3. Review the discussion of Romans 12:1-8, and apply it to your life. What do you feel are your strengths? What gifts has God given to you? What are you *not* gifted to do, and how can you team up with someone else who is strong in that area? (Hint: Try offering your strengths to those whom you look to for help in your own life.)

4. What do you feel are some of your optimum capabilities in life? List at least one gift, passion, and experience in life that have shaped you. Now write out at least one example where your gifts, passions, and experience overlap.

5. As you look to the future, what adjustment can you make to maximize the amount of time you spend either developing or using your optimum capabilities to serve others? Remember, you may need to team up with others first and give up something so you are freed up to really focus on your optimum capabilities.

6. Write a short summary below of God's unique calling on your life. How and where do you feel He is leading you to serve, in light of your God-given passions, gifts, and experiences?

TAKE BACK YOUR LIFE!

Choice #1:   Stop Climbing
Start Down the Ladder to Success

Choice #2:   Let God Be God
Build the Ultimate Alliance

Choice #3:   Don't Barter with Love—Give It Away
Make Love Your Gift and People Your Priority

Choice #4:   Serve Your Way to Success
Nurture a Servant Spirit

Choice #5:   Chase a Better Dream
Capture God's Vision for Life

Choice #6:   Build a Life-Team
Never Tackle Life Alone

Choice #7:   Play to Your Strengths
Stop Trying to Do It All

Choice #8:   Improve Your Flex-ability
Be a Lifelong Learner

Choice #9:   Slow Down and Focus
Do One Thing at a Time

Choice #10:   Nurture Sanctified Stubbornness
Keep the Faith No Matter What

WARNING:
*Pride says,
"I know my way."*

TAKE-BACK TIP #8
Humility says, "Lord, teach me more."

IMPROVE YOUR FLEX-ABILITY

Be a Lifelong

Learner

At Evangelical Free Church of Fullerton, we have a new members' class for people who want to join the church. This class provides people with an opportunity to get to know more about the church and how they can get involved. Whenever I visit this class, there's a question I ask to everyone in attendance: "How many of you want to join the church because you like it?" So far, in all the classes I've visited over the years, I've received a unanimous show of hands. After all, why join a church if you don't like it? No one has ever said, "I'm here to join the church because I can't stand it."

After everyone in the class lowers their hand, I then say, "Here's my promise to you: Because you like this church the way it is, my promise to you is that I will change it." Upon saying that, the room suddenly gets very quiet. I can tell what everyone is thinking: *Huh? We just said we like this church. Why are you promising to change what we already like?*

After allowing a moment for my promise to sink in, I explain my apparent insanity. "Our church has been here for 50 years. How many of you would be joining this church if we still functioned exactly as we did when we started 50 years ago?"

Up to now, no one has ever raised a hand—no one today wants to join a church that hasn't changed in 50 years! I then point out the obvious: "You like it the way it is *today* because we changed it *yesterday*."

The Necessity of Change

Change for the better is a sign of life and health. That's why we should expect change and embrace it. Now, that doesn't mean we change everything. God is still our ultimate priority, as well as the clear and relevant proclamation of His Word. Our commitment to Christ, the mission of the church, and the core values of God's kingdom should never change. But while the message and mission of the church should never change, the methods must change continually if we hope to be in business for the long haul.

Now think about your life. If you are growing, you had better be changing. If you don't want to break, you had better learn to stretch, bend, and flex. Change is a necessary part of any growing venture. As new needs and problems arise, they call for new solutions. So change is a part of staying healthy and relevant. As we go through change, we might find it tough because we're so accustomed to and comfortable with the status quo. But if there's a valid reason for change and if it's done right, then in the long run it's not only for the best—it's essential.

Pride says, "My way is good enough."

The Danger of Inflexibility

The most important truth we can learn about change is that it needs to begin in the heart before it can happen anywhere else.

This is illustrated in Jesus' call for Levi (Matthew) to become one of the 12 disciples:

> *He [Jesus] went out and noticed a tax collector named Levi sitting in the tax booth, and He said to him, "Follow Me." And he left everything behind, and got up and began to follow Him. And Levi gave a big reception for Him in his house; and there was a great crowd of tax collectors and other people who were reclining at the table with them. The Pharisees and their scribes began grumbling at His disciples, saying, "Why do you eat and drink with the tax collectors and sinners?" (Luke 5:27-30).*

I'll point out right up front that there were two people in this account who showed flexibility. First, Levi left his business in order to follow Jesus. He turned his back on the lucrative franchise he had built. And second, Jesus was willing to associate with what we might call "the wrong crowd." The Jewish religious leaders disapproved of this and complained loudly. To understand their mind-set, it's necessary to realize that tax collectors back then were not as honorable as they are today. In Israel, they were usually Jewish people who had "sold out" to Rome, the occupying force at this time in Israel's history. The Jewish populace strongly resented Rome's authority and detested supporting the oppressive Roman government through taxes. What made matters worse was that tax collectors only had to give Rome a certain amount and were allowed to keep whatever other money they were able to extract from the people. So in the eyes of many, Levi was an extortioner and a traitor. And here was Jesus, hanging out with this despicable tax collector and the scoundrels who hung with him.

Jesus responded to the Pharisees and scribes by declaring, "It is not those who are well who need a physician, but those who are sick. I have not come to call the righteous but sinners to repentance" (verses 31-32).

Now, Jesus wasn't saying that the Pharisees were righteous. He frequently condemned them as hypocrites who looked great on the outside but had some real problems on the inside (see, for example, Matthew 23:25-28). Rather, Jesus was acknowledging that the Pharisees, who considered themselves righteous by their own standards, didn't see their own desperate need for a Savior. They thought their good works gave them the inside track with God. It is those who know and admit they are sinners who realize their need for a Savior—and it was these people Jesus came for. When Jesus called the corrupt tax collector Levi to follow Him, Levi recognized his spiritual need and made a solid decision to follow Jesus.

The Pharisees made their contempt obvious and protested,

> *The disciples of John often fast and offer prayers,*
> *the disciples of the Pharisees also do the same,*
> *but Yours eat and drink. And Jesus said to them,*
> *"You cannot make the attendants of the bride-*
> *groom fast while the bridegroom is with them,*
> *can you? But the days will come; and when the*
> *bridegroom is taken away from them, then they*
> *will fast in those days" (Luke 5:33-35).*

In essence, Jesus was saying, "You guys don't get it. You don't understand the times we're living in, and you don't understand that the Son of God is in your presence. You're missing out on what God is doing. You're making a big fuss over My participation in a party with sinners, but that's not the real issue." Jesus then drove home His point with a parable:

> *No one tears a piece of cloth from a new garment*
> *and puts it on an old garment; otherwise he will*
> *both tear the new, and the piece from the new will*

not match the old. And no one puts new wine into
old wineskins; otherwise the new wine will burst
the skins and it will be spilled out, and the skins
will be ruined (verses 36-37).

In other words, when you use a new piece of cloth on an old garment, it won't work as a patch. A new cloth will flex and shrink, whereas an old cloth will have lost its ability to adapt and shrink. The two won't work together. They just won't match, and the next time the garment is washed, the patch will shrink and rip away from the older garment and ruin both the patch and the garment. Jesus was saying, "Some lives are like an old garment that has lost its ability to flex."

FOR GOD TO BE ABLE TO POUR NEW LIFE... MEANS WE CAN'T BE LIKE OLD WINE-SKINS THAT ARE RIGID AND THAT REFUSE TO CHANGE.

And when you pour new wine into a wineskin, the wine is still fermenting and "growing"—that is, it is still expanding. A new wineskin is supple enough to expand along with the fermenting wine. But if you were to pour new wine into an old wineskin, which has become brittle and hardened and dry, it will burst because it can no longer expand to accommodate the life that's in the new wine.

Jesus' point is that new wine requires flexible wineskins. And He was talking about the new wine of the gospel, the new wine of what God was doing through Jesus Christ, the new life that Christ was offering. God was about to do things in the midst of the Jewish people that would require them to stretch. Jesus was telling the Pharisees, "You're like old wineskins. You are too rigid to receive the blessings God wants to pour into your life."

When it comes to the life of the church and the methods we use in our ministries, we need to stay flexible. People change. Our culture constantly changes. Our churches should never become so set in their ways that they miss new opportunities to reach out and share the Good News with creativity. The message and the mission should never change, but our methods must be free to change for the church to stay relevant and effective with the next generation. That's flexibility.

So it is with our individual life. If we want to take back our life and make it all that God intends, we must nurture our flex-ability. For God to be able to pour new life, new wine, into our life means we can't be like old wineskins that are rigid and that refuse to change.

Humility says, "Lord, teach me more."

In our service to the Lord, we must nurture a flexibility that is willing to go along with the flow of change. How can we cultivate flexibility so God can keep molding and shaping us?

The Keys to Flexibility

Guarding Your Heart

In Proverbs 4:23 we find the exhortation, "Watch over your heart with all diligence, for from it flow the springs of life." Life flows from the heart, which is why humility is so important. And why humility keeps coming up in this book. Humility fosters flexibility.

By way of illustration, let's consider the physical human heart for a moment. One of the top killers in America today is heart disease. Many people die as a result of the arteries in and around the heart becoming hardened from a buildup of plaque and cal-cium deposits. We know from research that one way to prevent heart attacks is to keep our hearts soft and flexible, doing all we can to prevent that dreaded "hardening of the arteries."

This is true in the spiritual realm, too. We need to keep our hearts flexible so that we can stay healthy over time. Humility helps clear the heart of that dangerous hard plaque. Humility says, "Lord, change me. Teach me. Show me a better way." But if we are proud, our hearts will become inflexible and resistant to changes God wants to make in our lives. Taking back your life requires a flexible heart of humility.

When you read the New Testament, it becomes very apparent the Pharisees and scribes were always hung up on outward appearances and resistant to change. They learned to look good and put up a great false front, but their hearts were hard and cold. And Jesus said it's the heart that matters most to God.

What about us today? Are we abiding by certain routines or behaviors because we're concerned about what other people will think? Are we living life to please others, or to please our heavenly Father? Are we set in our traditional ways, or are we open to radical change, if necessary, to take back our life and offer it to God, flexible and ready to be used?

Jesus broke with tradition and followed the call of His Father to live with purpose and reach out to the lost. He demonstrated flexibility and a willingness to break with the norm of His day and drop into a party with the "wrong crowd." His participation did not mean He endorsed their lifestyles. He did not compromise His holiness, and neither should we compromise ours. But we do need to possess a heart that's flexible and softened by compassion. So this week, go to the party hosted by the "Levi" of your neighborhood, or better yet, ask him and his wife over for dinner!

Getting back to the broader issue at stake here, the biggest problem with the Pharisees and scribes was *prideful contentment.* They were satisfied with the status quo. They weren't thinking in terms of reaching outside their own circles. By contrast, God wants us to live with what I call a *holy discontentment.* By that I don't mean we should be discontent with our money and material things. Rather, I'm talking about being discontent with the status quo in our life. We should always be seeking new and better ways to tackle life.

How can we put this into practice? How can we keep our

hearts and lives soft and flexible, ready to receive new wine from God?

Keeping Your Heart Flexible

Here are four steps we can take to guard our hearts from a spiritual "hardening of the arteries":

ENJOY JESUS

Scripture repeatedly talks about Christians experiencing the joy of the Lord, but you almost wouldn't know about that because of the way so many Christians grumble and complain. Jesus came

PRAYERFULLY DREAMING WITH GOD WILL NURTURE FLEXIBILITY.

so that we might have joy and that our "joy may be made full" (John 15:11). The apostle Paul speaks to us of being filled "with all joy" (Romans 15:13). Joy is one of the fruit of the Spirit in our lives (Galatians 5:22). We can even know inner joy in the midst of our tough times (James 1:2). Yet all too often we're uptight and seemingly unable to relax with our Lord and simply enjoy life. That's not what God intended. If you're not enjoying the Christian life, you're not living it as God designed it. If you want to find out more about the joy we should experience as Christians, I recommend you read John Piper's book *Desiring God,*[14] or the short version, which is titled *The Dangerous Duty of Delight.*[15]

DREAM NEW DREAMS

We already mentioned dreams in an earlier chapter, but I want to affirm that a key part of staying flexible is dreaming new dreams and prayerfully pursuing Spirit-led, Word-inspired goals. Every now and then we should take time to sit quietly with God and do an inventory of where we are in life and where we want to go. We should establish goals for change and improvement in our spiritual growth, marriage, friendships, ministry, work, and any other important aspect of our life. And as you set fresh goals, focus on one or two really big dreams you want to work toward—and let them motivate you onward to greater growth. If you dream it, it may not come true. But if you fail to even dream it and ask God to bless it, I know it will never come true. Prayerfully dreaming with God will nurture flexibility as you seek to take back your life.

LIVE BY KINGDOM VALUES

As you endeavor to stay flexible, allow the values of God's kingdom to direct you. Listen for the *voice* of God, pursue God's *vision* for your life, and live by the core *values* of His kingdom. If you don't, you may end up flexing in ways God never intended you to flex. You may end up changing something that should never change. When God's values are your compass in life, you'll have restraints that help keep you from making tragic decisions. As you set goals and consider your options, remember this:

*The best change happens
when you first decide what you will
never change.*

If you firm up what you will never give up, then you are ready to flex, to make healthy changes, as you take back your life. This is the kind of flexibility you want to nurture—a flexibility that functions within God's values. You should flex, but never to the extent that you end up compromising your obedience to God and His Word.

BE A LIFELONG LEARNER

Decide from this day onward that you are going to learn something new every day of your life. Look for new things God wants to teach you. If there's something you've never done but always felt you should do, make this the year you step out in faith and just do it!

Three ways you can make sure you remain a lifelong learner are ...

- *Every month, read one good Christian book.* You'll be surprised at how much you'll grow and change as you allow yourself to be challenged by one good book per month. Read it slowly, asking the Spirit of God to show you how it should make a difference in your life.

- *Every week, meet with one good friend who encourages you, sharpens you, and makes you think.* Find a mentor who can stretch you and be stretched by you. Wisdom for life says, "Iron sharpens iron, so one man sharpens another" (Proverbs 27:17). In the same way that a physical trainer helps an athlete stretch for competition, we must help one another expand our flexibility.

- *Every day, spend time alone with God.* Read God's Word, and pray. Ask Him each day where He wants you to flex and grow. This requires the discipline of solitude in our lives. I really believe that God loves you and wants to show you where and how to flex your life. God wants to guide us as we make changes to restore order and balance and control to our life. But to do so, we need to first just BE QUIET! Create daily moments of solitude during which you sit alone with God and His Word. Ask God to speak, and I believe He will bring to your mind what He wants to change.

One of the most vital and creative mentors in my life has been seminary professor Dr. Howard Hendricks. I'll never forget a statement he made over 30 years ago: "The day you stop growing is the day you start dying." Be a lifelong learner. Keep expanding your dreams and horizons. When you stop, you begin to die. It is the nature of life.

Always Giving, Always Expanding

One of Howard Hendricks's heroes was an elderly woman who loved Christ dearly. Every time she saw Howard, she asked him, "Hey, Prof, have you read a good book lately?" She was always reading, always growing, always expanding. When she went to be with her Lord in her late 80s, she passed away in her sleep, and the next morning, those who found her saw two things on her bedside table: an open Bible that she had been reading, and a piece of paper on which she had just written down her new *ten-year goals*. Now that's the way God wants us all to go out! That's flexibility. Remember, old wineskins have nothing to do with our number of years on planet Earth. No matter how old you are, you never have to become an old wineskin.

CHOICE #8: IMPROVE YOUR FLEX-ABILITY

Chapter Summary: Get the Big Idea

We live in a rapidly ever-changing world. The stress created by the changes constantly taking place around us put incredible pressure on our life. How can we find our balance in the midst of such turmoil? First, decide what will never change, and commit to those unbending core values in life. They will help anchor your soul and simplify your choices. But also, stay flexible and open to change whenever possible, whenever change doesn't compromise your faith and convictions. Be a lifelong learner, always seeking wisdom and believing that GIFWMY—God Isn't Finished With Me Yet!

Questions to Guide Discussion and Your Choices

1. What heart attitudes caused the religious leaders of Jesus' days to become like "old wineskins"? What do you learn for your life from the parable about the wineskins?

2. How can contentment, the feeling that "good is good enough," become your enemy and stunt your growth? (Hint: Think of both your spiritual life and your relationships.) What are some areas in your life in which you want to keep learning and growing?

3. Review the section "Keeping Your Heart Flexible" on pages 160-162. Why do you think it is important to "enjoy Jesus"? What disciplines in your spiritual life help you keep the joy of following Christ?

4. What are some of the core values for your life that you should never change or give up, no matter what changes in your culture? List them and share them with your family or friends.

5. In an effort to be a lifelong learner, set the goal of reading at least one good book per month that will nurture your flexibility and growth. What book will you read first?

6. Remember, God will not be finished with us until we meet Him face to face. So determine to meet with Him daily, listen to His Word, learn from Him, and share with Him in prayer. You need His wisdom as you seek to take back your life. Complete this statement: My plan for meeting with my Lord daily this year is...

TAKE BACK YOUR LIFE!

Choice #1: Stop Climbing
Start Down the Ladder to Success

Choice #2: Let God Be God
Build the Ultimate Alliance

Choice #3: Don't Barter with Love—Give It Away
Make Love Your Gift and People Your Priority

Choice #4: Serve Your Way to Success
Nurture a Servant Spirit

Choice #5: Chase a Better Dream
Capture God's Vision for Life

Choice #6: Build a Life-Team
Never Tackle Life Alone

Choice #7: Play to Your Strengths
Stop Trying to Do It All

Choice #8: Improve Your Flex-ability
Be a Lifelong Learner

Choice #9: Slow Down and Focus
Do One Thing at a Time

Choice #10: Nurture Sanctified Stubbornness
Keep the Faith No Matter What

WARNING:

*Pride says, "Hurry,
you must do it all!"*

TAKE-BACK TIP #9:

*Humility says, "Slow down,
and focus on what's important."*

SLOW DOWN AND FOCUS

Do One Thing

at a Time

Florence Chadwick was born in 1918 and started swimming at a very young age. By the time she turned six, she was already a good distance swimmer. At age ten, she became the first child to swim the San Diego Bay Channel. A few years later, she became the first woman to swim the English Channel both ways. And on July 4, 1952, she determined to swim the 20-mile distance from Catalina Island to the coast of California.

Florence got an early start that morning. Even though it was July 4, the water was cold, the weather was chilly, and a heavy fog hung in the air. Partway into her journey, some curious sharks began to follow her. From time to time the people in a nearby boat—including her mom—would fire gunshots into the water to scare off the sharks.

The cold and fog persisted, and eventually Florence lost track of her time and distance. As the hours passed, her muscles became sore and felt as if they were burning. Anxious, she began to get confused and wondered if she could make it. She asked her mom if she could climb into the boat, but her mother said, "No, you can do this. Stay at it." After a while longer, Florence began to cry and thought she would drown if she didn't stop. At that point she was hoisted into the boat. Shortly afterward, she looked over the bow of the boat to the east and the fog lifted just enough that she could see the California shoreline. She was only about half a mile from the beach. She had swam for 15 hours and 15 minutes, and she had quit just short of her destination. Florence was very upset when she realized how close she had come to the shore, only to quit. Later, when she was interviewed, she said with regret, "I would have made it if I could have seen the shore, but all I could see was the fog." Florence had not lacked stamina. She had lost her focus.

The Value of Focus

Florence's experience illustrates well the importance of having a clear focus anytime we want to achieve a goal. A clear view of where you are headed is necessary when you tackle a major challenge. It's true in the world of sports, in academics, in business, in parenting, and in our personal life. If we can't see the finish line, then we get confused, distracted, and sometimes even give up. So in anything God calls you to do, a clear vision is essential. You must learn to focus and concentrate your energy and efforts on the goal.

The Bible has a lot to say about this, with one particularly powerful example in 1 Corinthians 9:24–27:

> *Do you not know that those who run in a race*
> *all run, but only one receives the prize? Run*
> *in such a way that you may win. Everyone*
> *who competes in the games exercises self-*
> *control in all things. They then do it to receive*
> *a perishable wreath, but we an imperishable.*
> *Therefore I run in such a way, as not without*

aim; I box in such a way, as not beating the
air; but I discipline my body and make it my
slave, so that, after I have preached to others, I
myself will not be disqualified.

In ancient Rome, the victors in athletic competition were crowned with a wreath. They worked hard for a perishable honor that shriveled up just a matter of days after the contest. By contrast, as Christians, we're in a race of far greater consequence. The prize we are pursuing is imperishable, and will last for eternity. And in order to know success, we need to run "as not without aim" and box "as not beating the air." In other words, we need to have a clear aim in view. If we don't, we certainly won't win, and we may not even finish the race.

Our need for focus is an important part of descending the ladder toward real success and life as it's meant to be lived. One of the main reasons people fall off ladders is a lack of focus as they descend. In fact, most tragic falls happen on the way down, not on the way up! So as we proceed downward, we want to make sure we don't lose our focus.

The Influence of Focus

Now this whole matter of focus is not limited to just one rung on our ladder. It affects all the rungs. Let me illustrate as I review some of the steps we've already taken since we began our descent.

Let God Be God—Focus on Christ

In all that we do, a constant focus on Christ is necessary or we won't remember to surrender to Him daily and let Him call the shots in our life. When we don't focus on Him, we're likely to forget Him and all that He has promised to us as His children. We need to focus and remember these five Ps:

- His *passion*—He loves us deeply
- His *presence*—He is with us always

- His *power*—He enables us sufficiently
- His *provision*—He meets all our needs
- His *promises*—He can be fully trusted

In light of these great truths about Christ and His presence in our lives, it just makes sense to focus on Him!

Make Love Your Gift—Focus on People as Your Priority

We live in a selfish world. Everyone is out for themselves. Yet Scripture commands us to love our neighbor—that's part of the Great Commandment. Jesus was the ultimate example, giving of Himself so that we might know salvation from sin. Love gives away to others without expecting anything in return. Focus on loving as a gift, not a wage or a bribe.

Serve Your Way to Success—Focus on Others

The next rung down our ladder to success is *service,* or a call to live as a servant with a focus on others. As Jesus said in Matthew 20:26, "Whoever wishes to become great among you shall be your servant." A servant heart is essential in every part of life—whether we're talking about our marriage, career, family, ministry, or anything else in our lives. "How can I serve you?" is the critical question to ask if you want to take back life as it's meant to be. Whether you are leading or following, to be great is to be a servant.

Chase a Better Dream—Focus Forward

As Paul says in Philippians 3:13, we're to forget "what lies behind." We're to focus forward and dream about what God can do in us and through us. And don't forget that God can "do far more abundantly beyond all that we ask or think, according to the power that works within us" (Ephesians 3:20).

When we realize that God dwells in us and that He can produce great results in us, then we ought to be dreaming of that which could be. We should never settle for yesterday's accomplishments. Do you have any clear and compelling dreams for your life, your marriage, your business, your church? Until you get them into focus, you won't reach them.

Build a Life-Team—Focus on Family and Friends

Team is the next rung downward. Remember that greater things are accomplished as we move forward together, never traveling alone. Life is built on relationships. As Hebrews 3:13 says, we are to "encourage one another day after day, as long as it is still called 'Today.'" There's more strength and wisdom in numbers. We all need others to cheer us on when we're tempted to quit. Life is not a solo sport, but a team effort. So focus on the vital relationships in your team.

Play to Your Strengths—Focus on Your Unique Giftedness

As part of a team, you need to specialize. You want to focus on your unique area of giftedness rather than attempt to do everything. As each person focuses on doing his or her part, everyone is built up. In 2 Timothy 1:6 Paul reminded Timothy, "For this reason I remind you to kindle afresh the gift of God which is in you." All of us are uniquely gifted by God to contribute in some way to the team. And the more you focus on your area of giftedness, the better life will go in every dimension. You can do more on less when you work from your God-given gifts. That takes focus.

Improve Your Flex-ability—Focus on Change

Flex is the next step downward on our ladder. We need to be open to fresh opportunities and ideas. We need to stay teachable to other ways to get the job done—at home, at work, in our ministry, and in our personal life. As Jesus said, you don't pour new wine into old wineskins (Luke 5:36-37). You can't force new ideas and opportunities into old molds. You need to be ready to flex, which means being a lifelong learner. You need to be ready to ask, "Lord, what do You want me to learn today?"

You see, every step of the way requires focus.

The Cultivation of Focus

How can we learn focus in a world that's so full of distractions? We have so many things competing for our attention—especially in this age of modern technology—that it's difficult for us to stay focused and accomplish significant goals. There are many "little things" that combine to eat up a big chunk of our day—cell phone calls, text messages, voicemail, e-mail, and countless other interuptions.

How can we maintain our focus in the midst of distractions that pull us in all directions? Paul tells us in 1 Corinthians 9:24-25, "Run in such a way that you may win. Everyone who competes in the games exercises self-control." That's our answer: We need to practice self-control. Take charge and focus on what's really important. As we learned earlier, when we try to do everything, we run the risk of doing nothing well.

If we run without aim, we will go nowhere. As Paul said, "I run in such a way, as not without aim; I box in such a way, as not beating the air" (1 Corinthians 9:26). In other words, you want to make sure you're running toward the finish line. Or in the case of boxing, you want to take aim at your target before taking your punches. Running or boxing with no clear goal will simply waste your energy.

I'll never forget a boxing match I saw in my high school gym class—a match that illustrates well the power of focus. A big, tall student was put into the ring with a small, short student. I thought the little guy was going to get clobbered, but the big fellow was flailing blindly, closing his eyes as he swung at his opponent. The little guy just kept ducking out of the way and waited until the right moment presented itself. And it came—suddenly he aimed right at his opponent's jaw, and boom! He leveled him. While this modern-day Goliath had every physical advantage, he wasn't taking aim, and it led to his downfall. The shorter David-sized student waited, got a clear view of his target, and concentrated all his energy in one blow.

That's how we need to live life—with careful aim and focus.

The Loss of Focus

There are several ways we can easily lose our focus in the Christian life. The apostle Paul tells us what they are in 2 Timothy chapter 2.

Distraction

Distraction comes easily for us, doesn't it? Paul wrote, "Suffer hardship with me, as a good soldier of Christ Jesus. No soldier in active service entangles himself in the affairs of everyday life, so that he may please the one who enlisted him as a soldier" (2 Timothy 2:3-4). The point here is not that the soldier stops living everyday life, but he doesn't get entangled in it. He doesn't allow himself to get bogged down in things that prevent him from giving his full attention to his calling.

> MAYBE YOU'RE NOT SEEING ANY RESULTS NOW, BUT IF YOU KEEP AT IT, THEY WILL COME.

So when you are at work, work with a single focus. But when you come home, do all you can to leave the work behind. When you are with the kids, be a great dad or mom, and when you are alone with your spouse, set your mind and heart on him or her.

Discouragement

Another way we lose our focus is through discouragement. Paul wrote, "The hard-working farmer ought to be the first to receive his share of the crops" (verse 6). After you've worked hard for results, it's pretty discouraging to not enjoy the fruit of your labors. Every farmer knows the four Ws of farming: work, water, weed, and wait. They know that they have to work faithfully day after day with no results. And in time, if they've done what they should do, they will reap a reward. God promises that faithfulness will be rewarded, so hang in there! In Galatians 6:9 Paul said, "Let us not lose heart in doing good, for in due time we will reap if we do not grow weary." Maybe you're not seeing any results now, but if you keep at it, they will come.

Disqualification

Yet another way we lose our focus is when we attempt to avoid the necessary steps to success by taking shortcuts or breaking the rules. That cannot be done in athletic competition, as Paul reminds us: "If anyone competes as an athlete, he does not win the prize unless he competes according to the rules" (2 Timothy 2:5). Either you follow the rules, or you're disqualified. And this is true in the Christian life, too. We live in a universe that has moral principles that cannot be broken without negative consequences. Those moral principles are designed not to punish us, but to help us succeed. And when we don't abide by them—when we don't follow God's principles—we will suffer consequences. We need to keep our focus and chase our dreams without compromising our loyalty to the Lord and His Word.

The Pursuit of Focus

Using the metaphor of a runner once again, Paul tells us how to keep our focus: "Run in such a way that you may win" (1 Corinthians 9:24). Now take care to notice what Paul does *not* say. He's not saying there is just one winner in the Christian life. He doesn't say you're racing against other Christians and only one can win the gold.

Remember that as you follow Christ, you are competing against yourself. God has given you unique goals designed just for you, and He wants you to pursue them to the best of your ability. You are to run so as to win. Don't be satisfied with just making the team. Run as if you were going for a gold medal. This is a call to excellence and away from mediocrity.

Even if your life seems somewhat out of your control, you can take it back. But it will take focus. It will require making tough choices on a daily basis. Here are three examples:

Choose your race and finish line carefully. In other words, make sure you have the right goal in mind. For example, if you were to swim from Catalina Island to the California coast, you would want to aim for Los Angeles, not Santa Barbara. Otherwise you would go far out of your way. Our world constantly tries to distract us and entice us to chase the pleasures of this life. Don't get off track.

How can we stay focused? Pay attention to the voice, vision, and values of God. Listen to His *voice,* His Word, and His Spirit within. Pray for His guidance and wisdom. Pursue God's *vision,* not the world's shallow and temporary versions of happiness. *Value* what your heavenly Father values, and live accordingly. For example:

- *Value the eternal over the temporal*—Why should we waste our time worrying about things that are not going to last? If you're running for the things that are temporal, then you're going to get a temporal prize, which, in time, will perish. Jesus said we're to lay up treasures in heaven. We're to value the eternal over the temporal, which includes valuing people over possessions.

- *Value the important over the urgent*—You need to decide what few things are truly important in life and focus on them, rather than trying to keep up with all the "urgent" tasks everyone else wants you to do right now. Protect your time. Keep your top priorities at the top of your to-do list. Don't let the less-important matters eat away at the time you need for that which really counts.

Seek God's approval rather than man's applause. Who are you trying to please? That's a great question to ask yourself if you feel your life is out of control. If you seek God's approval only, then your focus will stay constant. You will want whatever it is God wants. But if you live for man's applause, your focus will be

> **LIFE IS THE STAGE AND WE ARE ALL PLAYERS, AND GOD IS THE ONLY AUDIENCE THAT MATTERS.**

changing constantly. That's because everyone has different expectations and demands. You can't make everyone happy—nor should you try to. God is the one whom we must live to please. Life is the stage and we are all players, and God is the only audience that matters. So play to an audience of One, and your life will begin to come back into balance.

Realize we're all running different races, but the finish line is the same. Every Christian is running a different race. Your race is not my race; your calling is not mine. Every one of us is uniquely gifted to fulfill different roles and chase different goals. We're to excel at what we do, and not compare ourselves to others. Don't try to run someone else's race. Notice that world-class athletes almost never compete in more than one sport or one event. They compete so as to be the very best and win the prize. That requires enormous dedication and a singular focus on their unique areas of giftedness. As I said earlier, play to your strengths.

Though we're all running different races, we're all headed toward the same finish line, which is to hear God say, "Well done, good and faithful servant!" (Matthew 25:21 NIV). We all want that prize, don't we? We're all running our own race, and yet we all have the same goal—to please God and serve Him well.

The Elements of Focus

There's no quick or easy formula for running the race so as to win. It takes determination and persistence. Here are some practical tips:

Focus on Jesus Alone

Again, don't compare yourself to others. Look to Jesus as the standard. He is the measurement, the means, and the motivation of real progress. He is the *measurement* because the goal is to become like Christ. He is the *means* of getting there because it's by His Spirit that you live the Christian life. And He is the *motivation* because it's His love and grace that compel us to never quit. We love because He first loved us.

Work Hard

No athlete wins on natural ability alone. You can't win a race without training for the event. The best athletes work hard at what they do. Excelling at anything requires a constant, strenuous effort and tremendous sacrifice. The same is true when it comes to running the spiritual race and competing in the game of life. We are to "work out [our] salvation with fear and trembling; for it is God who is at work in [us] (Philippians 2:12-13). We are to work while remaining dependent on God's Spirit and power within us.

> TIME IS PRECIOUS, AND WHEN WE WASTE IT, THERE'S NO WAY TO GET IT BACK.

Exercise Self-control

You won't grow spiritually if you don't learn to practice your spiritual disciplines, which include worship, prayer, reading God's Word, serving, and giving. Similarly, world-class athletes put themselves on strict exercise and eating regimens. They don't skip workouts or eat whatever looks appealing, because they know that to do so will harm their bodies and hamper their ability to compete. To keep your focus sharp, you need to guard your spiritual health—and that means staying disciplined at whatever helps to build you up spiritually.

Protect Your Time

Ephesians 5:15-16 says, "Be careful how you walk, not as unwise men but as wise, making the most of your time." Time is precious, and when we waste it, there's no way to get it back. So you have to choose carefully how you're going to spend your time.

You can either use your time in a way that supports your focus, or in a way that diminishes it.

In my book *How to Lead & Still Have a Life,* I present what I call the four Rs of time, which can help us make the most of this precious commodity. You don't have to be a leader to benefit from these; you'll find them useful no matter what you do. Think of your day and its many activities in terms of four types of time. You need focused time for all four in order to be both healthy and productive in life. Here's a brief summary of them:

REST TIME

We all need rest time. In fact, God's Word tells us to rest for one day each week and do no work. When we take care of our health, we are better able to maintain our focus. During our rest time, we should focus on our spiritual health, marital health, and anything else that helps to refresh us. Scripture says we are to "work six days, but on the seventh day you shall rest" (Exodus 34:21). Give yourself one day of rest that is dedicated to worshiping your Lord, restoring your soul, and refreshing your vital relationships.

RESULTS TIME

Set aside some large blocks of time devoted to doing your "main thing"—whatever it is God has called you to do. These are the priorities that grow out of your unique role in life and the job God has called you to do. This is time set aside for the important people in your life and the pursuit of your truly important goals. It is here that you will know the greatest sense of fulfillment. Don't let life's many "little things" encroach upon this time. Set aside time to fulfill your calling, and protect it diligently. Interruptions are deadly to productivity, so use technology to protect you. Let the machines take the message. Let the cell phone tell your callers you can't take their call right now and that you'll call them back. Remember, your technological devices should serve you, not the other way around. Don't be a slave to them; let them work for you.

RESPONSE TIME

This is the time you can use to take care of all the "little things"—answering e-mails or phone calls, doing errands, and so on. These are the interruptions that frequently rob you of "results time." So set aside time for these distractions and use it solely for that purpose. That will help protect your vital "rest time" and critical "results time." Think of interruptions such as picking up trash in a room. It's quicker to put down your work, get out a broom, and sweep it all into a pile, then pick it up and dispose of it. Don't do it one piece at a time all day long while trying to get rest or work for results.

The key to this approach to time is to avoid, as much as possible, mixing these first three types of activities. When you've set aside time to rest, you should really rest. Focus on your rest time and refuse to pick up any work during that time. When you're doing something important, your main thing, then focus on it and don't try to rest or respond to little interruptions.

Keep in mind that most of us have at least two different worlds in which to apply these principles. On the job, this approach can dramatically increase our productivity and help us take back our life. And when we come home, we can apply these same principles to loving and caring for our spouse and kids. They are to become our "main thing." We are to safeguard our time at home for those whom God has called us to love and nurture.

Whatever the setting, the general principle is this:

Always know, wherever you are, what it is you must get done and do well. Then set aside dedicated, uninterrupted time to do it with excellence.

Now we're ready to look at the fourth type of time we all need—"refocus time."

REFOCUS TIME

This is a special time that you set aside about once a month—for part of a day or even a full day—to get alone with God and ask, "Lord, where do I need to change the way I'm investing in my *rest* time, my *results* time, and my *response* time?" This is time dedicated to prayerfully assessing how you are doing as a mom or dad, husband or wife, parent or child, on the job and at home. What should you be changing?

MAKE SURE YOU GIVE YOUR MAIN CALLING AND YOUR FAMILY THE BEST OF YOUR TIME.

Life is fluid, and you need regular opportunities to refocus on everything that matters in life. As you evaluate your priorities and ask for God's guidance, you'll get a better sense of what adjustments need to be made on a month-by-month basis. And as you let go of the nonessentials in your life, you'll be freeing yourself up to have more time to focus on that which really matters. This refocus time is when you, in a very real sense, take back your life before it gets out of control.

By the way, when it comes to making the most of your time, it's vital that you set your priorities because if you don't, others will. Plan your day in advance, and devote the best part of the day to that which matters most. And make sure you give your main calling and your family the best of your time. Don't give them the leftovers.

The Benefit of Focus

We all need greater focus if we hope to experience the life God designed for us to live. Life is not a perfect science. It is more art than science. And we struggle when our priorities get out of whack. So take time to assess your situation, give yourself some grace, and then get back into the race. Remember Florence Chadwick and her failed attempt to swim from Catalina Island to the California coast? She could have accepted defeat and spent the rest of her life regretting her decision to quit when she was so close to the finish line. But she didn't. She was a woman of focus. Two months later she was back in the cold water, and once again the fog was thick. But this time she didn't allow the fog to distract her. She later told a reporter that she focused on the vision of a beach, and she swam a straight line all the way to the Los Angeles shore. She completed the swim in 13 hours and 47 minutes, which was two hours faster than the previous record. She wasn't stronger this time around; rather, she was more focused.

That's what focus can do for you. When it comes to running the race called life, we need to make the main thing the main thing and let go of everything else. And when we do, we can know with certainty that after we cross the finish line, we will hear our Lord say, "Well done, good and faithful servant."

CHOICE #9: SLOW DOWN AND FOCUS

Chapter Summary: Get the Big Idea
One old proverb puts it this way: If you aim at nothing, you'll hit it every time. To get life under control and back into balance, we must learn to focus. This is done by choosing wisely, focusing on the target, and then concentrating on "landing the punch." If not, we will exhaust ourselves and fail to accomplish the important things in life. We will be flailing and failing as we try to take back our life. Focus your time and energy on the four Rs of life: rest, results, response, and refocus. Choose your focus and land your punches where they should go!

Questions to Guide Discussion and Your Choices
1. We all fail at times to stay focused on what really matters in life. Life is full of distractions. What are some of the major distractions you need to stay on guard against in your life?

2. Maintaining focus is important for every choice presented in this book. Review the focus required in previous chapters as you make the choices that shape your life. Where do you tend to lose your focus? Why?

3. Often overlooked and underappreciated is our need for quality *rest time*. It is God's will, modeled in creation, that we work six days and rest one. Why do you find it hard to take a day off for rest? Get creative and set aside one 24-hour period per week to restore your body, mind, and soul for the coming week. Write your plan now.

4. *Results time* protects undistracted blocks of time for you to do what matters most. What can you change in your work habits to apply this principle? What can you change in your home life to apply this principle and enhance your marriage and family time?

5. *Response time* is important as you seek to serve others and get back to them. What time will you set aside for responding to others? Remember to try, as best you can, to separate this from your rest time and results time. Remember to apply this to your work and your home life.

6. We all need *refocus time* because life is always changing and success is a moving target. Where and when will you regularly get alone with God and seek His wisdom for evaluating your priorities? Adjusting your plan?

TAKE BACK YOUR LIFE!

Choice #1: Stop Climbing
Start Down the Ladder to Success

Choice #2: Let God Be God
Build the Ultimate Alliance

Choice #3: Don't Barter with Love—Give It Away
Make Love Your Gift and People Your Priority

Choice #4: Serve Your Way to Success
Nurture a Servant Spirit

Choice #5: Chase a Better Dream
Capture God's Vision for Life

Choice #6: Build a Life-Team
Never Tackle Life Alone

Choice #7: Play to Your Strengths
Stop Trying to Do It All

Choice #8: Improve Your Flex-ability
Be a Lifelong Learner

Choice #9: Slow Down and Focus
Do One Thing at a Time

Choice #10: Nurture Sanctified Stubbornness
Keep the Faith No Matter What

WARNING:
Pride says, "Believe in yourself."

TAKE-BACK TIP #10:
*Humility says, "Lord,
my trust is in You."*

NURTURE SANCTIFIED STUBBORNNESS

Keep the Faith

No Matter What

At age 26 I became a pastor. I had been trained to dissect the Scriptures and teach them with relevance and enthusiasm. I had been trained to lead our church in outreach and discipleship ministries. But no classroom lecture could have prepared me for the events that would lead to my first funeral.

The story is real. Too real to forget. Only the names are changed. Mary was a vibrant follower of Christ. Fresh to the faith, it was all new to her and she loved it. She would sometimes get so excited about her relationship with Jesus that she would let a word or two of her old language leak out in the midst of her passionate prayers. No one cared that she used an occasional four-letter word in prayer because we knew her heart was overflowing with joy and love for Christ. She had three beautiful young children and a husband who was a great guy, but who did not share her faith.

One morning she left home on her bike, purse and tennis racket in hand, to meet some friends at a country club for a game of tennis. No one knows for sure what happened—something, perhaps her purse or racket, got tangled in the bike spokes, and in an instant she was flipped headfirst to the sidewalk. One bad bump to the head was her only injury. She would never go home to her family again. All through the next week, I sat every day with Mary's dear husband and her parents in the hospital. At first the doctors were optimistic, "She should wake up in a day or so." But unseen swelling continued, placing more and more pressure on her brain. As the days and nights passed with many prayers but no improvement, we all wondered, "Why?"

My first funeral was one I'll never forget. Sometimes life makes no sense and God appears to just not care. When life gets cruel and God seems distant, silent, and unconcerned, can you keep the faith? To take back your life requires perseverance. I like to call it the "sanctified stubbornness" of faith. It is a faith that stands strong in spite of the circumstances, not because of them. To take back your life and hold on to it for the long haul, you will need such stubbornness.

Expectations and Real Life

Life isn't easy here on planet Earth—which is why it's the ideal place to learn this art of perseverance. No matter what our place in life, we've all had to learn to endure through tough times. Because we live in a fallen world, trials have a way of finding us all. No one is immune to life's difficulties. So we must learn to keep the faith, no matter what! If we hope to take back our lives and keep them, we will need sanctified stubbornness of the soul. In a single word, we need perseverance.

Perseverance, simply defined, is the ability to endure without losing hope in the face of obstacles. It's an essential trait if we're going to know success in life. For example, every dad and mom has to learn to persevere when it comes to parenting. Children aren't easy to raise. If we hope to equip them to someday leave the nest and face life on their own, we must impart to them a faith that hangs tough under pressure. Every child has to learn to persevere when life kicks them in the gut, things don't go their way, or their dreams don't come easy. Every student has to learn to persevere in order to get that degree or that career. Every worker has to learn perseverance so he or she can get the job done.

Life often surprises us and tests our perseverence—through tough marriages, painful breakups, serious illnesses, financial difficulties, job losses, broken dreams, and the loss of loved ones. For example, one of my closest friends, who ministers on the staff of Campus Crusade for Christ, recently lost his college-age son, who was engaged to be married and had planned to enter the ministry. But he was killed in Afghanistan when his vehicle hit a land mine. The explosion took his life and the lives of three others. My friend is holding on to his life and his faith, but it isn't easy.

When we face tragedies like that, how do we learn to persevere in our faith? How do we endure with joy? We can be certain that for all of us, life on planet Earth will be a losing proposition in one way or another because of the presence of sin. We cannot escape the consequences of living in a fallen world, surrounded by fallen people, in bodies that are fallen and falling apart. So how do we persevere?

A Reality Check

The apostle Paul was very frank about what life will be like for us. We will all face times when we feel as though we're being pushed to the breaking point. Listen to his words of warning about suffering and hope:

> *I consider that the sufferings of this present time are not worthy to be compared with the glory that is to be revealed to us. For the anxious longing of the creation waits eagerly for*

> *the revealing of the sons of God. For the cre-*
> *ation was subjected to futility, not willingly,*
> *but because of Him who subjected it, in hope*
> *that the creation itself also will be set free from*
> *its slavery to corruption into the freedom of*
> *the glory of the children of God. For we know*
> *that the whole creation groans and suffers the*
> *pains of childbirth together until now. And*
> *not only this, but also we ourselves, having*
> *the first fruits of the Spirit, even we ourselves*
> *groan within ourselves, waiting eagerly for our*
> *adoption as sons, the redemption of our body.*
> *For in hope we have been saved, but hope that*
> *is seen is not hope; for who hopes for what he*
> *already sees? But if we hope for what we do not*
> *see, with perseverance we wait eagerly for it*
> *(Romans 8:18-25).*

Notice some of the key phrases in the passage:

- "the whole creation groans and suffers"
- "we ourselves groan within ourselves"
- we are "waiting eagerly for...the redemption of our body"
- "with perseverance we wait eagerly"

Romans 8:18-25 is what I call a good news-bad news passage. Let me give you the bad news first:

The Bad News Is...

> We all live on a fallen planet,
> in a fallen body,
> surrounded by fallen people,
> with an enemy who hates us.

We all live on a fallen planet—The earth on which we live has been corrupted by sin. It is not the ideal planet that God created, and it is not the planet that will be our restored home in eternity. Someday God will destroy heaven and earth as we know it and recreate a new heaven and earth in which we will dwell with Him forever, free of all sin and pain. *But we're not there yet.* So expect pain while on planet Earth.

We live in a fallen body—Our bodies are affected by sin as well. We age and fall apart with the passage of time. All you need to do is take one look in the mirror and compare it with a picture from your youth. Someday the Lord will deliver to us a new, resurrected, and restored body, free from illness and pain and death—forever! But look again in the mirror—*you're not there yet.* So expect some pain from head to toe and don't complain!

We're surrounded by fallen people—Everyone around us is a fallen creature who is susceptible to sin and fully equipped to hurt others. Therefore, we can expect to be hurt or treated unfairly. Even those who are Christians, who are being recreated in the image of Christ, have a long way to go (as you and I do) and will hurt or disappoint us from time to time. Someday, when we are in heaven, all our fellow believers will be perfect and loving 24/7. *But we are not there yet.* So expect, at times, to be wounded by the words and actions of others.

We have a spiritual enemy who hates us—First Peter 5:8 says, "Your adversary, the devil, prowls around like a roaring lion, seeking someone to devour." Satan is an intelligent spiritual being who wants to do everything he can to make us stumble and fall. Our culture is shaped by the Evil One and his deceptive lies about life. Someday, Satan will be bound and destroyed, never again to harass or hurt or destroy our lives. But again, look around—*we are not there yet.* So expect opposition from the enemy.

The Good News Is...

Then there's the good news, which Paul declares right at the beginning of Romans 8:18-25: "I consider that the sufferings of

THE GLORIES OF HEAVEN WILL FAR OUTWEIGH ANYTHING WE'VE ENDURED HERE ON EARTH.

this present time are not worthy to be compared with the glory that is to be revealed to us" (verse 18). In Christ, we are promised...

> abundant life,
> full joy,
> and a future glory
> that surpasses all the pain.

No matter how much pain and suffering the world throws at us, it's nothing compared to the great future waiting for us in eternity. The glories of heaven will far outweigh anything we've endured here on earth. And even as we walk through this life, Christ promises us peace and joy in the midst of the toughest times we encounter. In John 15:11, Jesus reveals His intention: "That My joy may be in you, and that your joy may be made full." Jesus spoke of full joy even on the way to the cross!

Perseverance and the Expectation of Pain

One problem many Christians have today is they've been shielded from much of the pain in this world, and they've somehow come to expect that their life in Christ will be free of suffering. There are even some who teach that all Christians are supposed to be healthy and wealthy, and that there's something wrong with us if we encounter problems in our life. But that's simply not true. Jesus said, "In the world you have tribulation" (John 16:33), meaning we can be certain that tough times will come. And James adds, "Consider it all joy, my brethren, when you encounter various trials" (1:2). Notice he said *when* we face trials—not *if*. So hardship is a certainty on planet Earth.

Look around you. Isn't it pretty evident God allows the same kinds of painful circumstances in the lives of both Christians and non-Christians? Just because we're believers and we walk with Christ doesn't mean God will shield us from the reality of living in a fallen body, surrounded by a fallen people, in the midst of a fallen world. Pain happens, and it rains on the just and the unjust!

One of the keys to living the Christian life successfully is accepting the fact that we should expect pain and suffering. God originally made this world free of suffering and death. Yet it wasn't long before mankind rebelled against God, and our sin lead to the fallen state of this painful place we call home. The good news is that God has a plan to redeem and restore us, our souls, our bodies, and even our planet. There is a new heaven and a new earth coming, and all who know Christ as Savior will enjoy them and Him forever! But this planet and this life is *not* heaven or heavenly. That's where perseverance comes in. How can we become the kind of Christian who is able to endure without losing hope in the face of life's obstacles?

Perseverance and Our Spiritual Growth

Perseverance Requires We Acknowledge Our Weakness

The apostle Paul knew all about perseverance. He alone faced more hardships in his years of following Jesus than any several of us will face in our entire life. So he's well qualified to teach us about the powerful virtue of perseverance, which he describes in 2 Corinthians 12:7-10. To give you a bit of context before we read the passage, keep in mind that Paul had received, by supernatural revelation, most of the New Testament epistles to the churches. He was the divinely chosen and inspired author of much of our holy Scripture. That made him a pretty significant instrument of God as the church was being launched. And yet that didn't shield him from experiencing life's pains:

> *Because of the surpassing greatness of the revelations, for this reason, to keep me from exalting*

*myself, there was given me a thorn in the flesh, a
messenger of Satan to torment me—to keep me from
exalting myself! Concerning this I implored the
Lord three times that it might leave me. And He
has said to me, "My grace is sufficient for you, for
power is perfected in weakness." Most gladly, therefore, I will rather boast about my weaknesses, so that
the power of Christ may dwell in me. Therefore I
am well content with weaknesses, with insults, with
distresses, with persecutions, with difficulties, for
Christ's sake; for when I am weak, then I am strong.*

Why was Paul given this "thorn in the flesh"? So that he wouldn't become proud. As we've noted thoughout this book, humility is a key trait to possess if we want to go down God's ladder of success. And here, we see Paul acknowledging the benefits of being kept humble, of being weak. He is willing, even happy, to put up with insults, distresses, persecutions, and difficulties if it's going to let God's power and sufficiency go on display through his life. Are you able to say that? Can you be content with pain and suffering because it forces you to depend on God's strength rather than your own?

PERSEVERANCE IS ROOTED IN THE SOIL OF ACKNOWLEDGED WEAKNESS.

Perseverance, then, is rooted in the soil of acknowledged weakness. It requires that we admit to God that we cannot handle life alone...and that's okay. When we humble ourselves in this way, we come to realize our need for God's help, and that's exactly what God wants.

Have you ever noticed how, when we're successful, we usually become proud of ourselves? Success fosters pride, and God hates pride. It sets us up for failure and discipline and heartache. Our human weakness, combined with pride, makes for a dangerous and lethal combination. Why? Because it produces...

• denial

• defensiveness

• self-reliance

Pride, when faced with a tough road ahead, will say, "I'm going to handle this myself. I'm smart enough and strong enough to do this." We take control, and God quietly retreats to the backseat as we grab the wheel, push the gas pedal, and take off to save ourselves.

Yet when we combine human weakness with humility, we get the exact opposite results:

• denial turns to honesty

• defensiveness turns to acceptance

• self-reliance turns to dependence on God

Like Paul, we need to be honest about the reality of our life this side of heaven. We need to admit we are weak and we cannot handle life on our own. Like Paul, we need to accept our weaknesses and say, "I am well content" with my limitations and expect to encounter ups and downs in life. In doing that, we become dependent upon God rather than ourselves. That's why Paul was such a powerful Christian—he understood the value of acknowledged weakness. What resulted? True success with humility.

Perseverance Grows Stronger When We Exercise Our Faith

In the same way that a hard workout at the gym makes us physically stronger, the exercise of our faith builds our spiritual capacity. In other words, a "faith workout" is what enables us to develop perseverance, as affirmed by James:

> *Consider it all joy, my brethren, when you*
> *encounter various trials, knowing that the*
> *testing of your faith produces endurance. And*

let endurance have its perfect result, so that you
may be perfect and complete, lacking in nothing
(James 1:2-4).

This may seem hard to believe, but it's the trials and hardships of life that test us and make our faith stronger so that we "may be perfect and complete." And I'm not talking here about life's minor inconveniences. True exercise doesn't happen until we push our muscles past their comfort zone, past their peak ability. Only then can your muscles grow. If you use the same-weight barbells over and over again, and you exercise for the same length of time during every workout, what's going to happen? You won't see much change. The same is true in pumping up our faith. Unless we're tested and tried at new levels of endurance, we're not going to experience any real growth.

UNLESS WE'RE TESTED AND TRIED AT NEW LEVELS OF ENDURANCE, WE'RE NOT GOING TO EXPERIENCE ANY REAL GROWTH.

God wants to make you perfect and complete—and that requires you to persevere through suffering. Now you may be thinking, *Does this mean God enjoys making me suffer?* Not at all. Joni Eareckson Tada, a Christian woman who has spent most of her life in a wheelchair as a result of a diving accident when she was a teen, has a great perspective on this, which she offers in her book *When God Weeps:* "God permits what He hates to achieve what He loves."[16]

God loves to see His children healthy and strong. But to get us there, He allows pain and suffering. He's a good Father, and good dads don't keep their children away from all painful experiences. Of course we human dads would rather raise our children in an environment totally free of pain and disappointment. But then our children would never learn how to cope and deal with the real world, which is going to inflict all kinds of hurts upon them.

Similarly, God is equipping us to deal with the world around us. And the good news is that He stands by our side as we learn how to persevere.

That brings us to a key question: How exactly do we exercise our faith? Paul gives us the answer in 1 Thessalonians 5:18: "In everything give thanks; for this is God's will for you in Christ Jesus."

There's one word in that passage that makes it really tough for us to obey this command: "everything." When we see that word, immediately we think, *You mean I'm supposed to be thankful for the bad stuff in my life, too?* And this is where the strengthening of our faith comes in. It takes a real exertion of faith for us to get to the point where we can kneel before God and say,

> *Lord, I'm hurting in this trial. I don't like*
> *what I'm going through. But I want to thank*
> *You—by faith—for this circumstance. I don't*
> *know its purpose or why I'm going through it,*
> *but I'm confident You can use this for good in*
> *my life or for Your kingdom. I trust You.*

It's this kind of attitude Paul was talking about when he said, "I have learned to be content in whatever circumstances I am" (Philippians 4:11). That's also what James meant when he said, "Consider it all joy, my brethren, when you encounter various trials" (1:2). Note he didn't say that we are to feel joyful because of the trial itself. Rather, we can consider it all joy *in the midst* of our difficulties because our confidence is in God. Our faith assures us that He *will* work through the trial. So in the midst of the pain, we can rejoice. To have sanctified stubbornness is to grow and have a faith that refuses to quit.

Perseverance Matures into a Sanctified Stubbornness of the Soul

So far we've learned that perseverance is rooted in acknowledged weakness. Then it grows stronger as we exercise that new faith, stretching it beyond its comfort zone. Trainers call it "feeling the burn"! Over time, it matures into what I call a "sanctified

stubbornness of the soul." Now usually we think of stubbornness as a negative trait, but there's a sense in which it's positive,
too—we can be stubborn about the right things. For example,
it's good to be stubborn about following God even when you are
persecuted for doing so. It's good to be stubborn about resisting
sin no matter how wonderful the temptation. And it's good to
be stubborn about giving thanks no matter how difficult your
circumstances.

This sanctified stubbornness of the soul appears in the Bible.
Note the opening words of 2 Corinthians 4:16-18:

> *Therefore we do not lose heart, but though our*
> *outer man is decaying, yet our inner man is*
> *being renewed day by day. For momentary, light*
> *affliction is producing for us an eternal weight*
> *of glory far beyond all comparison, while we*
> *look not at the things which are seen, but at the*
> *things which are not seen; for the things which*
> *are seen are temporal, but the things which are*
> *not seen are eternal.*

When Paul stated defiantly, "We do not lose heart," he was
declaring that he and his companions refused to live *under* their
circumstances. Rather, they claimed the purpose and promises of
the Lord in the midst of their difficulties and chose to live *above*
their circumstances. They didn't let the problems of life pull them
down, for they knew that their problems were merely "light afflic-
tion" compared to the incredible wonders awaiting them (and us)
in heaven. They weren't living in denial of their problems. They
were embracing the reality that God was with them, loved them,
and had an incredible future for them in heaven. That's reality.

Years ago I heard an interesting parable about an old mule
and a farmer. The story illustrates well what I mean by "sanctified
stubbornness." Once upon a time, there was a farmer who owned
an old mule. One day the mule fell into an abandoned well. The

farmer came home and heard the old mule bellowing at the top of his lungs from the bottom of the pit. After carefully assessing the situation, the farmer realized there was no way he could get the animal out of the deep, dry well. Realizing the mule had seen its best days many years ago, and knowing the well was worthless as a source of usable water, he decided to kill two birds with one stone. He called his neighbors together and told them what had happened. He decided the wisest thing to do was to bury the old mule in the well, hence putting the mule out of its misery and eliminating the hazard of the abandoned well at the same time.

So, as the old mule continued to bray, the farmer began to haul dirt and shovel it down on the mule to bury it. Initially the mule went crazy, thrashing and braying even louder! But as the farmer and his neighbors continued shoveling and more dirt hit his back, the mule quieted down and relaxed under the barrage of dirt from above. He was about to accept his fate when he got an idea. With every new blow from the dirt, the mule would simply *shake it off*, and *step up* on the dirt accumulating beneath him. The farmer and his friends could not see into the dark well, but they were sure they were burying the old mule as they shoveled the dirt into the well.

"Shake it off and step up...shake it off and step up...shake it off and step up!" the old mule repeated to encourage himself. No matter how painful the blows or distressing the situation seemed, the old mule fought panic and just kept right on shaking it off and stepping it up.

You probably know where this story is headed! It wasn't long before the old mule, battered and exhausted, stepped victoriously over the wall of the well to his newfound freedom! The very dirt intended to bury him actually lifted him to freedom and life! His "burial" became his salvation as he stood on top of his own grave—dirty, bruised, but alive. He refused to accept his fate, and kept shaking off the dirt and stepping up. As a result, he had a new lease on life and one great story to tell around the barnyard for the rest of his life![17]

When we find ourselves "down in a well," so to speak, buried by our challenges, we can do what the mule did—we can shake it off and step up. God supplies the motivation and the means for shaking it off and stepping up. His Spirit lives within us to empower our steps and His Word gives us the promises we stand upon to get out of the well. Here are my top 12 Bible passages that help keep my hope alive no matter what I'm facing:

A DOZEN REASONS TO ALWAYS HAVE HOPE[18]

God is always with you.	*Hebrews 13:5*
God loves you as His child.	*Romans 8:15-16*
God proved His love for you at the cross.	*Romans 8:32*
God's power is available to you.	*Philippians 4:13*
God can exceed your highest expectations.	*Ephesians 3:20*
God understands you and your problem.	*Matthew 6:8*
God promises to supply all your needs.	*Philippians 4:19*
God's grace is sufficient for you.	*2 Corinthians 12:9*
God works all things together for good.	*Romans 8:28*
God uses trials to produce maturity.	*James 1:2-4*
God uses trials to display your faith.	*Philippians 2:15*
God's will is good, acceptable, and perfect.	*Romans 12:2*

What is wonderful about these 12 promises from God is that they *always* apply. They are true and can be trusted no matter what! As you meditate on them, or encourage others to do the same, hope comes alive as faith is focused on the unchanging fact of God's presence and power in the midst of the struggle. They breathe fresh life into life when all seems hopeless. To take back your life, you will need an endless supply of hope based on the real and undeniable presence of a God who really cares.

This list is not only valuable for personal reflection, it is a tool you can use as you team up with others on the journey of life.

Remember, life is a team sport, not a solo performance. God wants all of us to be agents of hope for our family and friends.

Perseverance Enables Us to Help Others

Not only does perseverance strengthen our faith, it also builds up the faith of others. When others see your perseverance in the midst of trials, hope becomes contagious—it spreads like a virus. Those who might otherwise give up in despair can be comforted and inspired by your example. Paul himself said that our afflictions can help others who suffer:

> *Blessed be the God and Father of our Lord Jesus*
> *Christ, the Father of mercies and God of all comfort,*
> *who comforts us in all our affliction so that we will*
> *be able to comfort those who are in any affliction*
> *with the comfort with which we ourselves are com-*
> *forted by God (2 Corinthians 1:3-4).*

So just how can you infect others with renewed hope? In my book *How to Lead & Still Have a Life,* I present four actions that bring hope alive when it is dying. Here's an acronym you will want to memorize as you seek to offer hope:[19]

H elp	Communicate *compassion*
O ptimism	Express *confidence*
P erseverance	Display *courage* and *commitment*
E xploration	Encourage *creativity* and encourage exploration outside the box

Help—You must communicate compassion. When you say to someone, "What can I do to help you?" it communicates that you care. That can mean a lot, and it might be enough to help get the other person back on his or her feet.

Optimism—You need to express confidence and belief that, with God's help, things can change. When someone tells you, "I can't take this any longer," you want to come alongside that person and offer encouragement. You want to say, "I'm going to pray for you because I believe you can make it. I'm not asking you to deny the pain, but I do believe that, with Christ's help, you can survive. I am optimistic that God can create something good out of your circumstance." By showing an optimistic attitude, you give others hope.

Perseverance—You must display courage and commitment. When you face trials head-on and allow God to do His work in your life, it causes others to realize that they, too, can do the same. Your courage and commitment will rub off on them.

Exploration—If the problem or challenge persists, you can restore hope by encouraging creativity. Look for new solutions beyond the avenues you've already explored. You can help others by saying, "Why don't we think creatively about this and see if perhaps there's a solution we haven't noticed yet?" Getting someone to explore the possibilities can help bolster their willingness to persevere a bit longer.

Perseverance and the Display of God's Power

Yes, life is tough and we can fully expect to face our share of trials. But if we acknowledge our weaknesses and exercise our faith, we can experience the power of God's Spirit and the encouragement of God's Word. As we trust in and abide in Christ, we can keep the faith. We can take back our life with a "sanctified stubbornness of a soul" that refuses to say, "I quit." And that, in turn, can inspire others to do the same.

So when you feel like quitting, hang in there. Yield everything to God, and humbly admit that you can't go it alone. And through your weakness, God will have the opportunity to display His presence, His power, and His purposes in your life. You can take back your life!

CHOICE #10: **NURTURE SANCTIFIED STUBBORNNESS**

Chapter Summary: Get the Big Idea
Hope is as essential to life as food, water, and shelter. When hope is gone, the game is over, even if there is time left on the clock. Life on planet Earth is neither easy nor pain free. So as we fight to take back our life and restore it to what God intended, we need to develop perseverance—a divine stubbornness of the soul. It comes not from shallow, spiritual hype but from real hope based on God and the promises in His Word.

Questions to Guide Discussion and Your Choices
1. We've all suffered from unrealistic expectations for life. Where do you think the church has failed to teach an accurate theology of suffering? How have your expectations of God been out of line with Scripture?

2. How does acknowledging our weaknesses actually strengthen us for life? What do you learn from the apostle Paul's example of his "thorn in the flesh"?

3. Faith is like a muscle—it grows stronger only when it is stretched. What has God used in your life to stretch and strengthen your personal faith? How has this experience or test prepared you for future challenges to your faith?

4. Reflect on the story of the old mule and the well. If you had to choose three truths from God's Word to help you "shake it off and step up," what would they be? Memorize those verses this week.

5. Take time to review the "Dozen Reasons to Always Have Hope." Notice how these reasons always apply, in both good times and bad. Choose today to commit them to memory. Write them down. Review them daily until they are memorized and available to you 24/7. After all, you never know when they will be needed next.

6. God calls us to be agents of hope, especially to our family, our friends, and to others on our life-team. Reflect on the four actions (HOPE) that energize hope. When, where, and with whom can you be used by God this week to deliver hope?

IT'S YOUR LIFE...
CHOOSE AND
GO LIVE IT!

You really can take back your life. But sometimes it takes a crisis to move us in a new direction, to overcome the inertia of everyday life. New choices don't come easy. Floyd Green, a financial planner from North Carolina, faced some of the tough choices we've talked about. He chose well, and took back his life. But it took a brush with death to motivate him to start choosing life.

Floyd was a great climber. He was moving up the ladder fast as his business expanded and his client list grew. He was good at handling other people's money and was rewarded for his work. Yet Floyd was not a workaholic. He was pretty good at limiting his hours, checking out, and going home. His family and his faith mattered to him.

The problem was, Floyd could leave the office but not the work. His business was always there, in the back of his mind, distracting him and calling for his attention. He felt the business couldn't go on without his personal touch. His life looked together on the surface, but in reality, things were not so healthy. He was busy, buried, and behind, but thought he had little to no choice in the matter. So he just picked up the pace and did his best to juggle all the demands on his life.

But on May 5, 1995, everything changed in an instant. Floyd and his wife were biking on the shoulder of the highway; he in front and his wife close behind. She remembers being surprised as the side mirror of a passing car clipped her elbow. Her surprise turned to horror as that car drifted off the road and slammed into her husband at full speed. Floyd was thrown across the hood, into the windshield, and onto the pavement. His head injuries were terrifying and life-threatening. A policeman at the site of the accident gave him little to no chance of living. He was airlifted to a hospital, and the doctors gave little encouragement to the family. If he lived, he could be in a vegetative state the rest of his life. Or he could recover. Only time would tell. Floyd's wife prayed and tried to keep hope alive even as her husband's brain struggled for life.

After days in a coma, Floyd began to wake up. On one occasion he looked into his wife's face and asked, "Where's my Day-Timer?" It's as if, even in a coma, his mind was focused on the business! As he recovered, he learned that his brain injuries left him some limitations. He couldn't focus and multitask as he had before the accident. His tolerance for stress was severely lowered. He met with his doctor and got the hard truth. "Floyd, here's the deal. You can go back to work, but you must not return to life as it was. The nature of your brain injuries are such that if you do, you will not be able to handle it. You must limit your work to 20-25 hours per week and lower your stress level."

Floyd was skeptical of the doctor's prescription for his life. Yet he soon learned the doctor was right! Floyd got it. As he thought about and prayed over his predicament, he realized things had to change. He needed to make a major shift in the way he ran his life and business. Of course, he wondered if the company could survive. He wondered if he could adjust and live off a reduced income. He made some tough choices and began to live out the principles we've been exploring all through this book.

As his health improved, Floyd soon discovered a whole new quality of life. And much to everyone's surprise, his company continued to expand. Floyd took back his life after losing almost everything.

Now fast-forward to January 2005 and the inaugural gathering of the Christian Financial Professionals Network (CFPN) in Orlando, Florida. Floyd was just one of a roomful of successful business leaders attending my seminar on life management (built on the core principles of *Take Back Your Life!*).

After listening to my seminar, Floyd approached me. "Dale, keep spreading this message. People can change and recapture life if they are willing to follow this practical and biblical approach to life and leadership. I am living proof it can work. It wasn't until after my accident that I realized I had created a business that demanded my presence. I had to change. I gathered my employees and declared, 'I've trained you to need me. So now I must train you to *not* need me. Things will be different from now on. I've got to build a team and entrust more of this business to you.' And I did.

"Dale, I chose to take the team approach and then focus on my strengths. I chose to let God be God and follow Him. I chose to give up climbing the ladder and instead focused on being a better servant leader. And guess what? At the end of that year, our company had a small decline but was still in business. Before long I was making more than before the accident, while working only half the amount of time. Most importantly, my life came back into balance. These principles really work in real life."

Floyd's story is one of many I've heard over the years. People in every segment of today's overworked and overstressed culture are feeling the pressure and looking for a better way out from under the pile called "life." Whether you are a stay-at-home mom trying to manage a household or a corporate vice president over thousands of employees, life's demands can easily take control. Whether you are herding sheep on a ranch or shepherding a congregation or church, you can feel overloaded and overwhelmed by the constant cries of the "sheep." I know that myself, because that was my life. But that has changed. Jesus modeled a better way. The Scriptures direct us onto a better path. Life was never meant to be lived at such a breakneck pace.

How do you slow down and take back the life God intends you to live? *One choice at a time.* These choices may not be easy, but they are all actions *you* can take. First, *stop climbing.* Real life, the good life, true success is never found by climbing faster and higher. With a spirit of contentment, stop the climb and change directions. Then start choosing life by doing the following:

Let God be God. He loves you and only He can help you really live on planet Earth and prepare for eternity at the same time. With humility, ask Him to assume the lead as you climb down the ladder toward life as it is meant to be.

Make love a gift and people your priority. The Great Commandment, loving God and loving people, is essential to great living. We all have a lot to learn about love. Make it your mission to be a lifelong student of the people God has brought into your life—your spouse, your kids, your associates at work, your neighbors and friends. All of us are in the people business 24/7.

As you love, humble yourself and *serve your way to success.* Jesus said to be great, be a servant. Ask, "How can I better serve you?" That is the question of the day, every day, in every arena of life. It is the secret to success from the bedroom to the boardroom.

Choose to *chase a better dream*—God's dreams for your life, your career, and your family. He loves you and will guide you if you seek Him and listen. Use His priorities to narrow your focus, and then concentrate on the pursuit of those dreams. The world will tempt you to try and *do* it all, try and *have* it all. Listen to the heart of God, set your sights on the right target, and go for it!

Build your life-team and begin to let others share the load.

Life is a team sport, not a solo race. If you want to take back your life, start by letting others use their strengths to serve you, as you return the favor. In your family, at the office, in your church... think team! What will you release to others this week?

Now start *playing from your strengths* as much as possible. None of us get to specialize all the time, but God has gifted you and given you passions for a reason. So begin to prayerfully focus on doing less of everything and more of your main thing. Life is more fun and you will be more effective as a mom or dad, as an employee or boss, as a servant in your church. It works to lead with your best stuff!

Choose to never stop learning. *Improve your flex-ability.* Changing your habits and patterns will not be comfortable at first. In fact, it may downright hurt. But to turn in a new direction will require learning, changing, and flexing as the world around you moves on. Forget the past. Every month, pick up one new book to enrich your life—at home, on the job, or in whatever ministry God has called you to pursue. Live in the past or lean toward the future—it's your choice!

Now, choose one thing at a time. *Slow down your pace and focus.* Look ahead this week and choose, decide for yourself, what really needs your time and attention. Don't let others rob you of time with the most important people in your life. Set aside time to worship and rest—one day every week. Set aside time to do what matters most in your job or at home. To fail to plan is to plan to fail! Choose today what you will never give up...time with your Lord, fun with your spouse, playtime with your kids or grandkids.

Last of all, nurture that sanctified stubbornness of the soul. *Keep the faith no matter what!* Choose your convictions and stick to them with the tenacity of a bulldog. No matter what life throws at you, focus on the promises and presence of your incredible Lord and Savior. He is always with you. He can always be trusted. He will always provide what you need. He is the One who declared,

"I came that they may have life, and have it abundantly" (John 10:10). Decide now, choose now, to fight for the life God intends for you as His child. Take back your life. And as you do, remember to give it over to Him so you never lose it again!

Ten choices you can make. Ten steps you can take. May the joy of a young child be yours again!

NOTES

1. Tim Kimmel, *Little House on the Freeway* (Portland, OR: Multnomah Publishers, 1988), p. 28. Used with permission.

2. Ibid., p. 28.

3. H. Dale Burke, *How to Lead & Still Have a Life* (Eugene, OR: Harvest House Publishers, 2004), p. 51.

4. Found on a UC Berkeley Parents Network page on the Internet at http://parents.berkeley.edu/jokes/toddlerrules.html (accessed on August 29, 2006). Author unknown. This list appears in varied forms elsewhere on the Internet.

5. Merrill F. Unger and R.K. Harrison, *Unger's New Bible Dictionary* (Chicago: Moody Press, 1988), s.v. "Humility."

6. Jim Collins, *Good to Great* (New York: HarperBusiness, 2001), pp. 12-13.

7. Martin Luther King Jr., "I Have a Dream," excerpted from http://www.usconstitution.net/dream.html (accessed on August 29, 2006).

8. Ibid.

9. Bill Thrall, Bruce McNicol, and John Lynch, *TrueFaced* (Colorado Springs: NavPress, 2003), p. 20. Used with permission.

10. Rick Warren, *The Purpose Driven Life* (Grand Rapids: Zondervan, 2002).

11. *The American Heritage Dictionary of the English Language* (Boston: Houghton Mifflin, 1973)—s.v. team

12. Ibid.—s.v. teamwork

13. Marsha Hornok, "Psalm 23, the Antithesis." Used with permission.

14. John Piper, *Desiring God* (Portland, OR: Multnomah Press, 1986).

15. John Piper, *The Dangerous Duty of Delight* (Sisters, OR: Multnomah Publishers, 2001).

16. Joni Eareckson Tada and Steven Estes, *When God Weeps* (Grand Rapids: Zondervan, 1997), p. 84.

17. Adapted from a story heard long ago; original source unknown.

18. Adapted from H. Dale Burke, *How to Lead & Still Have a Life* (Eugene, OR: Harvest House Publishers, 2004), pp. 222-23.

19. Adapted from *How to Lead & Still Have a Life*, p. 225.

To contact the author, write:

Dale Burke
℅ Harvest House Publishers
990 Owen Loop North
Eugene, OR 97402

You can also find out more about Dale Burke and Dale Burke Leadership seminars and resources at www.daleburke.com

Also from H. Dale Burke...

FINALIST FOR ECPA'S GOLD MEDALLION BOOK AWARD 2005

HOW TO LEAD

& Still Have a Life

The 8 Principles of
LESS IS MORE
Leadership

H. Dale Burke

Caught in the Vicious Cycle of

Busy, Buried, and *Behind?*

Every leader knows the feeling. You think that if you just work harder, faster, and longer, you'll eventually get on top of the pile. But no matter how hard you try, you keep falling further behind.

How to Lead & Still Have a Life will transform your leadership and your life, helping you to master...

Spirituality—the Power of Convictions

Humility—the Power of Servant-Leadership

Imagination—the Power of Vision

Mobilization—the Power of Letting Go

Specialization—the Power of Optimum Capabilities

Innovation—the Power of Creativity

Concentration—the Power of Focus

Determination—the Power of Hope

These disciplines transcend the ebb and flow of modern fads. In fact, they were modeled by Jesus Christ. And they'll empower you to both lead effectively *and* still have a life.